BE YOUR OWN GREENHOUSE EXPERT

Dr. D. G. Hessayon

1st Edition 200,000

Year:	Location:

pbi
PUBLICATIONS

pbi PUBLICATIONS · BRITANNICA HOUSE · WALTHAM CROSS · HERTS · ENGLAND

Printed and bound by BPCC Hazell Books, Aylesbury, Bucks, England

ISBN 0 903505 32 0

© D G HESSAYON 1990

CHAPTER 1

INTRODUCTION

How to use this book

On each page you will find scores of facts to help you with your plants. Check up each time you decide to buy or have a new job to do. On many of the pages there are sections which are printed in blue — these are for you to fill in with your own information. In this way you can build up a permanent record and a useful reminder for next year.

Perhaps the greatest joy in owning a greenhouse is the one which receives least attention in the textbooks. The point is that when you go through that metal or wooden doorway and then close the door, you are entering a private world which isolates you from your workaday worries as well as the weather.

Outdoors you must share your plants with neighbours, passers-by, family and so on, and all around you there is an environment you cannot control — frost, wind and rain dictate your activity. Not so in the greenhouse — all you have here are you, a protected environment and a group of plants which rely upon you for their very existence. Watering, feeding, pricking out, potting on ... without you they must surely die.

There is something very comforting about working in a well-run greenhouse. You are warm and dry when the wind is blowing or the rain is falling outside, and your results depend entirely on your skill rather than on the vagaries of soil type and weather. But don't be oversold by some of the glowing pieces in books, articles or catalogues.

First of all, greenhouse growing is not simply a matter of common sense — there is nothing obvious about the right way to train a Cucumber or the reason why you have to ventilate on a cool day. Do read books like this one and its companion volumes to find out what to do. Next, don't be fooled into believing that not much work is involved. Constant attention is needed at most times of the year, and this means every day in summer unless you install an automatic ventilator and an automatic watering system. Finally, take the money-saving claims with a pinch of salt. An average-sized heated house will certainly not "pay for itself quite easily in a year". The greenhouse fitted with staging etc will cost you about £300 and the fuel a further £100 a year to keep the temperature at a minimum of 42°–45°F during an average winter.

So it is not a money-making proposition nor is it a simple pastime calling for occasional action. It is instead an absorbing hobby which enables you to produce a range of plants at a time when their garden counterparts are far behind or their growth outdoors is impossible. There is a steady stream of jobs to do, but none of these is strenuous, which makes greenhouse growing especially suitable for the not-so-young and the disabled.

All sorts of shapes and a wide range of sizes are available, but the fundamental difference between one type and another is the minimum temperature at which it is kept. The cold house is the simplest — no artificial source of heat is provided and so in the depths of winter the temperature will almost certainly fall below freezing point. Despite this, the cold house extends the growing season by trapping the sun's heat during the day. Here you can work protected from the elements with plants which are sheltered from wind and rain and can enjoy day temperatures which are appreciably higher than outdoors. Tomatoes are the favourite crop — during the rest of the year there are cuttings to take, seeds to sow and vegetables to grow. You can have Strawberries, Turnips and Potatoes weeks before the outdoor crops are ready and a wide range of annuals can be grown to provide colour.

Still, the cold house is rather limited. You cannot grow frost-sensitive plants between early winter and mid spring unless you provide heat. The usual practice is to turn the structure into a cool house in which winter temperatures do not fall below 42°–45°F. A whole new world opens up because you can now grow 'greenhouse plants' — Azalea, Cineraria, Cyclamen, Freesia, Primula, Streptocarpus and many, many more. Half-hardy bedding plants can be raised for the garden and a succession of blooms can be created for either greenhouse or living room. The installation of a heater transforms growing under glass from a place for Tomatoes, Cucumbers and hardier plants into a place of great variety in which to exercise a year-round hobby.

So buy that greenhouse if you have the money to spare, enough free time to care for it properly and a liking for growing things. If possible, buy the next size larger than you have planned as most people who buy a greenhouse soon run out of space for all the exciting things they want to grow. Keep it as a cool house — the attraction of having a warm house with a minimum temperature of 55°F is obvious if you want to grow exotics, but such warm conditions are undesirable for some plants and you will also have a fuel bill of about £300 a year. The stove house with a minimum temperature of 65°F is for the tropical specialist and not for you.

What you grow is up to you. Perhaps you just want to produce fruit and vegetables with little thought for floral display. On the other hand you might want nothing more than blooms and foliage attractively arranged all year round — in this case your greenhouse has become a conservatory. Although there are no strict rules about what to grow, you should avoid trying to grow too varied a mixture — you cannot place shade lovers like Ferns next to sun lovers such as Geraniums. Finally, don't let your greenhouse become a place which houses a row of Tomato plants, an assortment of house plants which have finished flowering, a few trays of shop-bought annuals awaiting bedding out and a collection of pots, gardening equipment and household items. A greenhouse offers you a way to extend the joy of gardening — use it properly.

TYPES

TYPE A
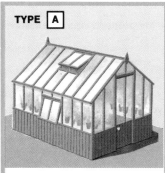
SPAN ROOF
The traditional style has vertical sides. Use of space and heat is efficient, and enclosed lower part cuts down winter heat loss. Choose an all-glass version for growing-bag and border crops.

TYPE B

DUTCH LIGHT
Sloping sides and an even span roof — angled glass makes it warmer and brighter than a traditional span roof house. Also more stable, but supporting upright plants from floor to roof is more difficult.

TYPE C
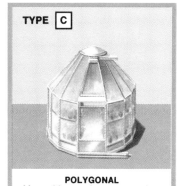
POLYGONAL
Many sides — six, seven or nine. Attractive when filled with pot plants and sited close to the house. Expensive, however, and not a good buy if you want maximum space for your money.

TYPE D
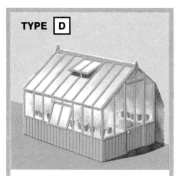
THREE-QUARTER SPAN
Lighter and more airy than a lean-to — useful for growing wall plants such as Grapes and Figs. Expensive, however, so the choice should be between a span roof house or a lean-to.

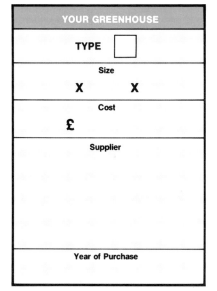
YOUR GREENHOUSE
TYPE
Size
X X
Cost
£
Supplier
Year of Purchase

TYPE E
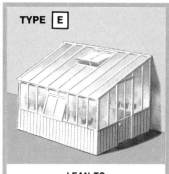
LEAN-TO
Useful for a south- or west-facing wall. Bricks store heat during the day — fuel bill is reduced. This is a usual pattern for a conservatory — an interconnecting door makes it part of the home.

TYPE F
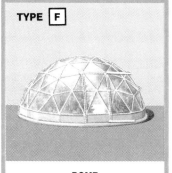
DOME
Three advantages — attractive appearance when filled with flowers, maximum stability and maximum light absorption. The major drawback is its unsuitability for growing tall crops effectively.

TYPE G
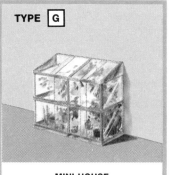
MINI-HOUSE
Very useful where space is strictly limited — a lean-to which will accommodate the plants but not you. Treat as a cold house, but small size can mean a very rapid rise in temperature in summer.

TYPE H

POLYTUNNEL
Plastic sheeting is stretched across a series of metal hoops — this is the cheapest form of greenhouse. Good for low-growing crops such as Lettuce and Strawberries, but not really suitable for Tomatoes and Cucumbers.

STRUCTURE

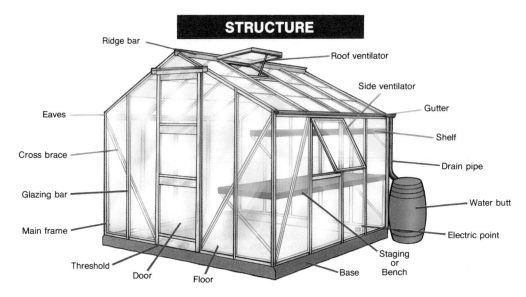

Ridge bar — Roof ventilator
Side ventilator
Eaves — Gutter
Cross brace — Shelf
Glazing bar — Drain pipe
Main frame — Water butt
Electric point
Threshold — Staging or Bench
Door — Floor — Base

STAGING & SHELVING

Benches or staging are essential if you grow pot plants — constant stooping to ground level would add backache to greenhouse gardening. The two terms are interchangeable in popular use, but strictly speaking staging is a permanent structure whereas a bench can be removed. The basic choice is between a perforated and a solid surface. Slatted wooden staging about 2½ ft above the ground is the traditional form. Air can circulate in winter, cutting down the risk of disease. Solid staging lacks this advantage, but it can conserve heat in winter. Shelving is a miniature form of bench which is secured at head height to house small pots or trays when space or sunlight is restricted. Nowadays you can buy metal benches and shelves as an optional extra. Collapsible types enable you to grow bedding plants and bulbs at a convenient height in spring and then you can dismantle the benches in summer to grow Tomatoes in growing bags. A portable potting bench is a good idea —use a wooden or metal tray with solid sides to hold compost, trays and pots when taking cuttings, filling seed trays etc.

WATERING EQUIPMENT

A can with a long spout is essential for watering individual plants. Watering is a time-consuming job which must be undertaken every day in summer. An automatic or semi-automatic system is essential if you cannot spare the time. There are 3 basic systems — capillary matting, capillary bench and trickle irrigation. See page 28 for details.

BLINDS

Plants must be protected from the sun's rays in summer. Blinds are one of the answers available — these are roller types with wooden slats, plastic slats or plastic-coated sheeting. These blinds are fitted either inside or outside the greenhouse — see page 33 for details. Automated fans are a useful luxury — these slatted blinds go up and down according to the temperature within the greenhouse.

HEATER

Some form of heating is necessary if you plan to grow half-hardy plants during the frost-prone months. See pages 30–31 for details.

THERMOMETER

A maximum/minimum thermometer is vital. Suspend it close to the plants but make sure that air can circulate freely around the thermometer. It should be close to eye-level at the north side of the house. There are 2 types — the traditional mercury thermometer with internal tiny iron bars which you set with a magnet and the new digital type which you reset by pressing a button. Make a note of the readings at frequent intervals.

GUTTERING

Guttering is a useful extra as rainwater dripping from the roof can undermine the foundations. Some models have built-in guttering as a standard fitting — check before you buy. The water from the gutters should be channelled to a soakaway or into a plastic water butt. The butt should have a tight-fitting lid to keep out leaves and other debris. Experts do not agree whether such water is safe to use for watering greenhouse plants — never use it if the water is obviously polluted.

FLOOR

The traditional pattern for the floor of the greenhouse was to have one or both sides as border soil for growing plants and a central pathway covered with pea shingle, concrete, concrete slabs or wooden slats (duckboarding). The pathway remains as important as ever (rammed soil is not satisfactory) but most experts no longer recommend using border soil for growing annual plants such as Tomatoes. The problem is a build-up of diseases and other problems in the soil. Growing bags and pots are preferred these days. If you plan to use the border soil, dig in 4 oz per sq. yard of Growmore plus a liberal amount of garden compost well before planting time. Do not plant the same crop in the border year after year. If you don't intend to have borders then concrete the whole area or cover the ground on either side of the pathway with shingle.

DOOR

Hinged or sliding — both types have their disciples. Sliding doors can be used as an extra ventilator and they don't slam shut. But hinged doors generally fit better. and so are less likely to be a source of draughts.

GLAZING

Buy **glass**. It is heavy and not as safe as plastic, but the advantages far outweigh the drawbacks. More light enters and it is easier to shade and clean. Of even greater importance is its ability to retain heat — in frosty weather the temperature inside the house will be about 8°F higher than outside. Buy 24 oz horticultural grade.

Polythene and **PVC** are the usual plastics, and both have a limited life. PVC is dearer, longer lasting and a little more heat-retentive than polythene. Use UVI grade polythene. Glass has one major problem — it will shatter if hit by a heavy object. If you are near the road or a play zone, consider **polycarbonate** sheet. It has some of the advantages of glass but it is light and unbreakable. Unfortunately it scratches easily and is more expensive.

Putty is no longer used for glazing — panes are bedded into mastic or a dry glazing system is used.

VENTILATORS

Hinged ventilator

Louvred ventilator

The ventilators on most standard models are inadequate. There should be at least one roof ventilator and one side ventilator — a single ventilator at the top of the house is not enough. The total ventilator area should be at least 20% of the floor area — this usually calls for one roof ventilator and one side ventilator for each 8 ft of length. Louvred ventilators are better than the traditional hinged type, but make sure that they close properly. Extra ventilators can be bought as optional extras — make sure that side ones are set low down to ensure proper air circulation. An automatic ventilator may be described as an 'optional extra' in the catalogue, but it is an essential if you take your greenhouse seriously and cannot spare the time to go out daily to open or close the ventilators. An extractor fan is another useful aid — see page 29 for details of these items of equipment.

INSULATION
See page 62 for details.

ELECTRIC POINT
A power point is essential if you are going to take greenhouse growing seriously. Even if you do not heat your house by means of electricity you may still need a 3-pin point for the propagator, winter lighting, extractor fan etc.

SIZE
A wide range of sizes is available. The standard sizes are from 6 to 20 ft long and widths of 6, 8 or 10 ft. The one you choose will depend largely on the money and space available — remember the annual cost of fuel as well as the initial outlay. The most popular sizes are 8 ft x 6 ft and 10 ft x 8 ft — choose the larger one if you plan to have staging on both sides. If you intend to grow Tomatoes the height to the eaves should be at least 5 ft and the ridge height about 7 ft. Somewhat surprisingly, it is more difficult to control the environment in a small house than in a large one. Increased size reduces the problem of draughts and sudden fluctuations in temperature.

FRAME
Aluminium alloy has taken over from wood as the most popular material for greenhouse frames. It is cheaper than wood, requires no maintenance and the thin glazing bars mean more light within the house. Warping of the ridge does not occur and re-glazing is a simple matter. There are several minor drawbacks. Aluminium greenhouses lose slightly more heat at night than wooden ones and condensation drips are more likely to occur. The metal frame is received in bits and so construction is usually more difficult than with a timber model. A white bloom occasionally appears on aluminium frames — this is normal and nothing to worry about. Frames with a white or bronze coating are available.

Wood is considered by many to be more attractive than metal, especially in an old world setting. There is no need to bore holes to attach staging, support wires etc — nailing or fixing hooks is a simple matter. Buy Western Red Cedar, Teak or Oak. Treat every few years with a water-based preservative or linseed oil. Pressure-treated softwood is cheaper — treat occasionally with Bio Woody. Untreated softwood is a poor buy — regular painting is necessary.

Galvanised steel greenhouses are no longer popular. They are heavy, hard to erect and rust can be a problem when the surface is scratched.

PROPAGATOR
Cuttings need a moist and reasonably warm atmosphere in order to root satisfactorily. Seeds of some important greenhouse crops, including Cucumber and Tomato, require a temperature of 60°–75°F in order to germinate properly. Obviously it would be ridiculous to create these conditions throughout the greenhouse — a heated propagator is the answer. A propagator is a plastic or aluminium container with a glass or transparent plastic cover. Choose one heated by electricity rather than by paraffin, and look for thermostatic control and one or more ventilators at the top of the cover. Make sure it is big enough for your needs. There are mini-greenhouses in which you can keep tropical plants in stove house conditions, but you will probably need something much simpler. There should be enough floor area for at least 2 seed trays and enough headroom to hold pots containing 6 in. high plants.

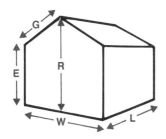

MEASUREMENT	CALCULATION	YOUR HOUSE
Volume	W x L x ½ (E + R) ▷	cu. ft
Surface area	2 x G x L + 2 x E x L + (E + R) x W ▷	sq. ft
Approximate glass area	95% of surface area ▷	sq. ft

Examples

Length (L)	Width (W)	E	R	G	Volume	Surface area	Approximate glass area
6½ ft	4½ ft	5 ft	7 ft	3 ft	175 cu. ft	158 sq. ft	150 sq. ft
8 ft	6 ft	5 ft	7 ft	3½ ft	288 cu. ft	208 sq. ft	195 sq. ft
8 ft	8 ft	5 ft	7 ft	4½ ft	384 cu. ft	248 sq. ft	235 sq. ft
10 ft	8 ft	5 ft	7 ft	4½ ft	480 cu. ft	286 sq. ft	270 sq. ft
12 ft	8 ft	5 ft	7 ft	4½ ft	576 cu. ft	324 sq. ft	305 sq. ft

CHOOSING

Greenhouses come in all sorts of shapes, sizes .... and prices. Choosing the right one is difficult, and if you make a mistake you will have to live with it for a long time. Take time before deciding. Look at the advertisements and study the catalogues carefully. But the best plan is to look at actual greenhouses — go to your garden centre, DIY store or large garden show like Chelsea or Southport.

● **IS IT THE RIGHT SIZE?**
Too big or too little — both pose a problem. The greenhouse should not dominate the garden, but it must be large enough for your needs. A popular (but not always correct) rule is to buy the next larger size to the one you first thought of.

● **DO I LIKE THE LOOK OF IT?**
Metal is cheaper, domes are trendy but above all — does it appeal to you? Remember that you have to live with it — it will be part of the garden display.

● **CAN I AFFORD IT?**
Making your own house from scratch is not an economical option these days. Be careful of 'bargains' — if funds are limited the best choice is an aluminium alloy house from a reputable supplier. Remember the fuel costs — there is not much difference between the various types, although electricity is usually the dearest.

● **IS IT RIGHT FOR THE USES I HAVE IN MIND?**
If you plan to concentrate on tall plants like Tomatoes and Cucumbers, choose a greenhouse with vertical sides and floor to roof glass. Half-timbered sides are suitable if you want to reduce fuel costs and you plan to grow pot plants only.

● **IS IT SOUNDLY MADE?**
Is the door wide enough for your width, and your wheelbarrow if you plan to work in the border soil? Do the ventilators and door fit properly? Is the ridge bar rigid and firmly made? Press the glazing bars — are they unyielding?

● **ARE ESSENTIALS INCLUDED IN THE PRICE?**
Make sure that essentials are not classed as 'optional extras' unless you can afford the additional cost. Check exactly what is included in the price. Glass, benches and an adequate number of ventilators are all essentials, but are not always included in the basic price. A foundation may be offered as an optional extra, but treat it as an essential feature. Make sure that you are told about any delivery or erection charges.

If you have marked 6 ticks, the house is ideal. Five ticks mean that you should think again — 4 or less mean that you *must* think again.

SITING & ERECTING

Planning permission is not usually necessary for an average-sized house in a standard location. It is still best to check — there may be rules about the distance from the boundary, and a lean-to attached to a house will need permission.

Most experts recommend that the house should be set so that the ridge runs from East to West. A few believe that the house should run North to South, but all agree that orientation is not a key factor for an average-sized house.

Do not site a glass greenhouse close to the road or a play area — replacing broken panes is always annoying. Other sites to avoid are waterlogged soils and frost pockets — never try to erect a greenhouse on recently-dug soil.

Site the greenhouse well away from trees — 30 ft is the recommended minimum distance. An overhanging branch casts shade, drops dirt on the glass below and may break off in high wind. Choose a sunny site, away from buildings which could shade out winter sun.

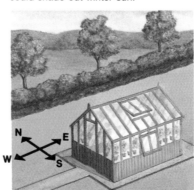

Foundations should not be required if the house is 8 ft x 6 ft or less. You will need a firm and level base. Buy the recommended foundation if offered by the manufacturer — follow the instructions exactly. Larger houses are generally set on concrete foundations.

A windbreak such as a hedge is useful on the North and East sides, as strong winds can damage the structure and even ordinary winds increase the heating bill. The greenhouse should be sited at least 10–15 ft away from the hedge.

Site the greenhouse as close as practical to the house — electric wiring is costly and carrying other forms of fuel to the far end of the garden is a chore in winter. If possible run both water and electricity to the greenhouse.

Read the instructions carefully before you start to erect the structure. Lay out the parts and number them if necessary. Wait for a still and dry day before glazing. Make sure the frames are square — never use the glass to straighten aluminium glazing bars.

CHAPTER 2

PLANTS

It is difficult to define what we mean by a 'greenhouse' plant. Some plants live their whole lives within the confines of the glass walls. Others provide their display or produce under glass but either start their lives or spend some time outdoors. The remaining plants have a life pattern which is just the opposite — they provide their display or produce in the garden but they start their lives or stay for a period in the protected environment of a greenhouse.

The first group described above are true greenhouse plants in every sense of the word — they spend all their lives under glass. Examples are the greenhouse varieties of half-hardy vegetables such as Eurocross Tomatoes and Telegraph Cucumbers. There are tender climbers like Hoya and Passion Flower, and greenhouse Grapes such as Black Hamburgh. No problem of classification here, but there are hundreds of plants which are house plants rather than greenhouse plants because they are more at home in the living room than under glass.

The second group is a small but important one — greenhouse plants which spend some time outdoors. Included here are the pot-grown late-flowering Chrysanthemums, pot-grown Strawberries and the bowls of bulbs which begin life in a plunge bed outdoors.

The final group is large and complex — garden plants raised or overwintered under glass. Not 'greenhouse' plants in any sense of the word, but half-hardy bedding plants, half-hardy vegetables, Chrysanthemum cuttings, bedding Geraniums and outdoor Tomatoes all use the greenhouse at a vital stage in their lives.

Bulbs
Plants which are reproduced by planting underground storage organs — true bulbs, corms, tubers etc. Some are tender **Greenhouse Bulbs** — others are hardy **Garden Bulbs** which can be grown outdoors.
Pages 8–10

Pot Plants
Greenhouse Pot Plants are non-bulbous plants grown for the sole or primary purpose of providing a decorative display within and not outside the greenhouse. Many plants are grown in pots under glass for other purposes, such as food production.
Pages 11–14

Bedding Plants
Plants which are raised from seeds or cuttings in the greenhouse and are then planted out in the garden as temporary occupants to provide a colourful display. Bedding plants may be annuals, biennials or perennials.
Pages 15–16

Garden Perennials & Shrubs
Plants which spend all their active adult lives in the open garden but occupy the greenhouse either at the start of their lives or during the winter months when frost threatens their existence.
Page 17

Tomatoes
For many years the most popular greenhouse plant and likely to remain so. Once grown in border soil and pots — now primarily cultivated in growing bags. Seed is sown in early March for planting in early May.
Pages 18–20

Cucumbers
Second only to Tomatoes in popularity. Once a difficult crop, requiring higher temperatures and moister air than Tomatoes, but new F_1 hybrids have made Cucumber cultivation much simpler.
Pages 21–22

Vegetables
Greenhouse Vegetables spend all their lives under glass, from seed sowing to harvest. **Garden Vegetables** are hardy or half-hardy varieties which are raised as seedlings under glass, prior to planting out in the garden.
Pages 23–25

Fruit
Plants which are grown solely or primarily for fruit production. Some, such as Melons and fan-trained Peaches, spend all their lives in the greenhouse — others live part of their lives in the garden.
Pages 26–27

Bulbs

A large number of plants grown in the greenhouse produce 'bulbs' which can be used for propagation. Sometimes these underground storage organs are true bulbs (fleshy scales surrounding a central bud), but others are corms, tubers or rhizomes.

This group of plants can provide you with colour almost all the year round, and most of them are easy to grow. There are two basic rules to remember. The first one is that you must buy good quality stock from a reputable supplier — how well a bulb flowers depends largely on the way it was grown and stored. The second rule is that you must not forget about the plants once flowering is finished. Keep them watered and well fed until the foliage has died down, and then store the bulbs as instructed.

Remember to buy bulbs which are recommended for indoor cultivation — some garden varieties of Tulip fail miserably in the greenhouse. If you want Hyacinths, Narcissi and Tulips for Christmas flowering then you should buy 'prepared' bulbs rather than ordinary ones.

Greenhouse Bulbs

These plants cannot tolerate frost and are never placed outdoors in winter. Most are summer- or autumn-flowering and they usually lose their leaves during the dormant period. Depending on the variety the bulb may be left in the pot during this time or it should be removed and stored in slightly moist peat.

Garden Bulbs

Many of the popular bulbs which flower in the garden during the spring months can be grown in the greenhouse. There are two basic growing techniques. The forcing method is used for large bulbs to make them bloom well ahead of their garden counterparts. The second method is used for smaller bulbs and is simpler than forcing, but flowering will only be a short time ahead of similar bulbs in the garden.

Greenhouse Bulbs

	Type grown
ACHIMENES: A. hybrida is available in many colours — trumpet-flowered plants much used in hanging baskets. Plant the small rhizomes ½–1 in. deep in early spring for summer and autumn flowering. Store rhizomes in dry peat. Re-pot every 3 years	
ARUM LILY: The Calla Lily in the U.S — Zantedeschia aethiopica in the catalogues. Upturned white trumpets on 3 ft stalks appear in spring. Reduce watering after flowering — store bulbs in peat for planting in August	
BEGONIA: Many spectacular tuberous Begonias are offered for sale — the giant-flowered B. tuberhybrida, the smaller B. multiflora and the pendulous B. tuberhybrida pendula. Plant tubers in 5 in. pots in spring. Lift tubers and store in peat at the end of the season	
CANNA: C. hybrida plants are big, bold and colourful. The large flowers are borne on a 2–4 ft stalk — there is a wide variety of both flower and leaf colour. Plant in spring — re-pot each year at the same time	
CRINUM: The lily-like flowers of C. powellii measure 6 in. across and the leaves are about 3 ft long. A magnificent display for late summer, but summer-planted bulbs will take several years to reach the flowering stage. Re-pot every 3 years	
CYCLAMEN: A great greenhouse favourite — swept-back flowers above silver-patterned leaves. Tubers are planted in summer for winter display — seed sown in June will take about 18 months to flower. Reduce watering when flowers fade. Remove corms or keep pot on its side until midsummer — re-pot using fresh compost, burying the tuber to half its depth. Keep cool — 50°–60°F is ideal. Many varieties are available — some scented	
EUCOMIS: The Pineapple Lily needs lots of space. The long leaves form a large rosette and the cylindrical spike of small white flowers bears a leafy crown. Plant the bulbs in a 5 in. pot early in the year — the flowers appear in midsummer	
FREESIA: The funnel-shaped flowers of F. hybrida grow on one side of the 1–1½ ft long wiry stems — choose from white, yellow, blue, lilac, orange, pink or red. Plant corms in summer — 6 per pot for winter flowering. Alternatively sow seed in early spring	
GLORIOSA: The Glory Lily bears large lily-like flowers in summer. Some form of support must be provided. Plant the tuber in spring with the tip about 1 in. below the surface — water sparingly at first. After flowering store tuber in its pot — re-pot in spring	

Achimenes hybrida English Waltz

Canna hybrida J B van der Schoot

Cyclamen persicum Decora

Greenhouse Bulbs contd.

	Type grown

GLOXINIA: The bell-shaped velvety blooms are 3 in. or more in diameter — a great greenhouse favourite for summer display. Plant the tubers in 5 in. pots in late winter or early spring — keep in a propagator at first. Water sparingly — more plentifully later but keep off leaves and flowers. Re-pot in spring

HAEMANTHUS: The Blood Lily is the popular variety — a ball-like flower head measuring 8 in. across appears in summer. Plant the bulb with its tip above the compost in summer. The plant is evergreen — water sparingly in winter and re-pot every 4–5 years

HIPPEASTRUM: The popular 'Amaryllis' is really a Hippeastrum hybrid. The funnel-shaped flowers are 5–6 in. across — the strap-like leaves appear at or shortly after flowering. Plant bulb in a 7 in. pot in late winter or early spring for summer flowering. Prepared bulbs are available for earlier blooming

HYMENOCALLIS: The Spider Lily is cultivated for its attractive sweet-smelling blooms which appear in late spring or summer. The flowers look like daffodils with long and narrow petals. Plant the bulbs in winter — may be listed as Ismene

IXIA: I. hybrida has dark-centred starry flowers on upright wiry stalks. Not common, but this bulb is nearly hardy so it can be planted early in the year in a cold house for flowering in early summer

LACHENALIA: The Cape Cowslip is an attractive plant with pendant yellow flowers tinged with red. Plant 6–8 bulbs in a 6 in. pot in late summer for winter flowering — the tips should be just below the surface — water sparingly until shoots appear. Re-pot in autumn

LILIUM: A number of Lily varieties can be successfully grown under glass, but choose with care. Popular types include the Mid-Century Hybrids — plant bulb in a 6 in. pot in autumn. Cover the tip with 1½ in. of compost. Keep cool, dark and moist. When shoots appear move to a brightly lit spot for early summer flowering

NERINE: N. sarniensis is the Guernsey Lily — narrow-petalled white, orange or red flowers crowded on 1½ ft stalks. Plant the large bulbs in August for winter flowering — make sure the tops are well above the compost. Keep in a cold frame until shoots appear — then water and bring into the greenhouse

SMITHIANTHA: The pendant flowers of Temple Bells are a blend of yellow, orange and pink. These appear in autumn above the mottled leaves. Plant rhizomes on their sides in late winter — re-pot each spring

SPREKELIA: Plant the Jacobean Lily in autumn for flowering in early summer. Once the red flowers have faded and the foliage has died down let the compost dry out. Keep cool until spring — bring into growth by watering. Re-pot every 3 years

TUBEROSE: The white fragrant flowers of Polianthes tuberosa appear above the grass-like foliage in winter — not a common sight in greenhouses. Plant the bulb-like rhizomes in spring — re-pot each spring

VALLOTA: In late spring plant the bulb of Scarborough Lily in a 5 in. pot — leave the top half of the bulb uncovered. The bell-like flowers are borne on 1–2 ft stalks in late summer. The leaves are evergreen — do not re-pot until the clump of bulbs becomes overcrowded

VELTHEIMIA: The Forest Lily is a good but unusual choice. Plant the large bulb in early autumn and about 4 months later the 1 ft flower stalk arises from the centre of the leaf rosette. This stalk bears about 60 small tubular flowers

Hymenocallis festalis

Lilium Destiny

Smithiantha hybrida

Vallota speciosa

Garden Bulbs

● FORCING TECHNIQUE
for Hyacinths, Tulips & Narcissi

Planting: Choose bulbs which are good-sized, disease-free and firm. Bulb fibre is sometimes used as the growing medium, but if you intend to save the bulbs for garden use after blooming then choose seed and cutting compost. Place a layer of moist compost in the bottom of the pot and set the bulbs on it. They should be close together but must not touch each other nor the sides of the pot. Never force bulbs downwards into compost. Fill up with more compost, pressing it firmly but not too tightly around the bulbs. When finished the tips should be above the surface and there should be about ½ in. between the top of the compost and the rim of the pot.

Care After Planting: The bulbs need a 'plunging' period of complete darkness and a temperature of about 40°F. The best spot is in the garden covering the pot with about 4 in. of peat. Failing this, place the container in a black polythene bag and stand it in a shed, cellar or garage. Any warmth at this stage will lead to failure. The plunging period lasts for about 6-10 weeks. Check occasionally to make sure that the compost is still moist.

Care During Growth: When the shoots are about 1-2 in. high move the pot into a shady spot in the greenhouse — under the staging is ideal. Conditions should be cool but frost-free. After 7 days move the pot to a bright and then to a sunny part of the house. The leaves will now develop and in a few weeks the flower buds will appear. Now is the time to move the pot to the chosen site for flowering. Keep the compost moist at all times. Provide some support for tall-flowering types. Feed with a liquid fertilizer.

Care After Flowering: Cut off flowers, not flower stalks. Continue watering and feeding until leaves have withered. Remove bulbs and allow to dry, then remove dead foliage and store in a cool dry place. These bulbs will not provide a second display indoors — plant in the garden in autumn.

● NON-FORCING TECHNIQUE
for other bulbs

Planting: It is essential to choose a container with adequate drainage holes. Place a layer of crocks at the bottom and add a layer of seed and cutting compost. Plant the bulbs closely together and add more compost. The tips of the bulbs should be completely covered.

Care After Planting: Place the pot in the garden.

Care During Growth: When the plants are fully grown and flower buds are present bring the pot inside to the site chosen for flowering. Treat in the same way as Forced Bulbs.

Care After Flowering: Treat in the same way as Forced Bulbs.

Daffodil
Large-cupped. King Alfred will bloom in Jan

Narcissus
Short-cupped. Many white and yellow varieties
plant: Aug -Oct
in flower: Jan -April

Jonquil
Small flowers. Tiny-cupped and fragrant

Early Narcissus
Several blooms on stem. Paperwhite will bloom before Christmas
plant: Aug -Sept
in flower: Dec -Jan

Early Single Tulip

Early Double Tulip

Darwin Tulip

Lily-flowered Tulip

The most satisfactory types for growing indoors are the Early Single and Early Double varieties. Darwin Tulips will need support
plant: Sept-Oct
in flower: Jan -April

Roman Hyacinth
Dainty blooms; slender stems. White, blue and pink varieties available
plant: Aug -Sept
in flower: Dec -Jan

Dutch Hyacinth
Large compact heads; strongly fragrant. Wide range of colours available
plant: Sept-Oct
in flower: Jan -March

Crocus
plant: Sept-Oct
in flower: Feb -March

Iris reticulata
plant: Sept
in flower: Jan

Scilla
plant: Sept-Oct
in flower: Jan -March

Snowdrop
plant: Sept-Oct
in flower: Jan

Chionodoxa
plant: Sept-Oct
in flower: Feb -March

Grape Hyacinth
plant: Sept-Oct
in flower: Jan -March

Varieties grown

Pot Plants

The reasons why plants are grown in pots in the greenhouse are numerous and varied. There are seedlings of bedding plants and vegetables destined for transplanting outdoors and there are cuttings of border perennials and shrubs for planting out later in the garden. There are fruit trees in pots, overwintering tender garden plants in pots and so on.

Greenhouse Pot Plants are a large but distinct group within this range of container-grown plants. The single feature that all of these non-bulbous plants have in common is that their sole or primary purpose is to provide a decorative display within and not outside the greenhouse.

The choice is enormous, but year after year the same mainstays remain — varieties of Chrysanthemum, Carnation, Pelargonium, Fuchsia, Cineraria, Primula, Impatiens and Begonia. Other popular ones include Calceolaria, Heliotrope, Salpiglossis, Schizanthus, Streptocarpus and a wide range of foliage house plants. Many are annuals which can be raised from seed — others are perennials which are propagated from cuttings. For the larger greenhouse there are shrubs (Camellia, Hydrangea etc) and climbers (Passion Flower, Jasmine and so on). Some specialist gardeners devote a greenhouse to a single group — Alpines, Cacti, Ferns or Orchids. Most of us, however, prefer a jumble of various Pot Plants, and with skill a colourful display can be created practically all year round.

Notes

Greenhouse Pot Plants

	Type grown
ABUTILON: Abutilon hybrids are attractive large plants, growing 5 ft or more. The pendant bell-like flowers are 2 in. long. These plants are best treated as annuals — sow seed in February for a summer display. If kept as a perennial stand the shrub outdoors in summer	
ALPINES: Rock plants are a good choice for the cold greenhouse. They don't take up much space and welcome the protection from winter rains. Mix coarse sand or grit with compost when re-potting and provide plenty of fresh air (not draughts) and some shading in summer. Grow in half pots. Suitable types include Lewisia, Aspenula and dwarf varieties of Anchusa, Campanula, Saxifraga, Thyme, Verbascum and Viola	
AZALEA: Countless Azaleas (Rhododendron simsii) are bought every year at Christmastime to provide decoration during the holiday season. It is not an easy plant to keep from one season to another. Keep cool and make sure the compost is moist at all times, using soft water. Stand the pot outdoors between June and late September	
BEGONIA: The types of flowering Begonia are many and varied, and identification is often difficult. The showiest blooms are borne by the tuberous types (see page 8) — described here are the fibrous-rooted ones. B. semperflorens (Wax Begonia) is the most popular one, raised from seed sown in February for a summer and autumn display. Lorraine Begonias are old favourites, blooming at Christmastime — they are raised from summer cuttings. Brightly-flowered Hiemalis hybrids such as Fireglow can be bought in flower at any time of the year	
BOUGAINVILLEA: Distinctly tropical climbers which produce brightly-coloured bracts throughout the summer. A fine conservatory plant which can reach the roof, but a minimum of 45°–50°F is required in winter. Keep almost dry during this dormant period	
BROWALLIA: A showy plant easily raised from seed — sow in early spring for summer flowering or delay sowing until summer for winter blooms. B. speciosa bears violet flowers with white throats. Pinch out growing tips occasionally to promote bushiness	
CACTI & SUCCULENTS: Their popularity continues. The strange shapes and colourful flowers of many of them appeal to plant lovers — the ability to cope with neglect appeals to gardeners who can't give their plants regular attention. Desert Cacti require no water at all between November and March — all you have to provide is a frost-free environment. Re-potting isn't often necessary and growth rarely gets out of hand. But summer care is needed — most types require normal watering and good ventilation. The Forest Cacti (Epiphyllum, Zygocactus and Schlumbergera) have special needs — see The House Plant Expert, page 100	

Abutilon hybridum Michael

Browallia major

Greenhouse Pot Plants contd.

	Type grown

CALCEOLARIA: The Slipper Flower is a springtime favourite. The soft leaves are large and hairy and the spotted pouch-like flowers are 1–2 in. across. It requires cool and airy conditions. Sow seed in late spring or summer — maintain a minimum temperature of 45°F during winter

CALLISTEMON: The Bottlebrush Plant is well named — the summer flower spikes look like red bottle brushes. The problem with this shrubby plant is that it can get out of hand — cut back all straggly growths in autumn. Take stem cuttings in spring

CAMELLIA: A fine winter-flowering shrub when grown in a large pot or tub. The single or double blooms, 3–5 in. across, appear amongst the glossy leaves. Not easy — the house must be a cold one and you will have to use lime-free water and compost. Stand the pot outdoors once flowering has finished and bring it indoors in autumn

CAMPANULA: C. isophylla is the popular one — a blue- or white-flowered trailer. The star-shaped blooms appear all summer long on plants grown from seed sown in March. Cut back the stems after flowering. C. pyramidalis (Chimney Campanula) is a tall upright plant with white or blue flowers

CAPSICUM: A popular annual grown for its colourful elongated berries which appear in winter and early spring — the display should last for 2 or 3 months. Sow in March or April — keep the compost moist at all times and mist the leaves frequently when the plant is in flower and fruit

CARNATION: Grow the Perpetual-flowering types — these are the ones you see at the florist shop. Choose a Sim variety — buy rooted cuttings in spring. Remove the tips to induce the formation of side shoots and move to a 5 in. and finally a 7 in. pot as growth proceeds. Provide adequate support for the long stems and remove the side buds to ensure large blooms. Cut flowers can be obtained at any time of the year if a minimum temperature of 50°F can be maintained. The plants will survive but not bloom at 42°F

CELOSIA: Sow seed of this feathery-flowered annual in February for a summer display. The yellow or red plumes remain attractive for many weeks provided you do not allow the compost to dry out. An odd form (C. cristata) with a velvety cockscomb head is available

CHRYSANTHEMUM: Greenhouse Chrysanthemums are the late-flowering sorts, producing blooms from October until late December. For large flowers choose an Exhibition variety and carry out the ritual of stopping and disbudding. The year begins in January or February when cuttings are taken — alternatively buy rooted cuttings in early spring. In April transfer the rooted cuttings from 3 in. to 5 in. pots. In mid May move into 8 in. pots and insert one or more stout canes to support the stems. Pinch out ('stop') the tips of the stems when they are about 8 in. high. In early June move the pots outdoors. Water regularly and at the end of September bring the pots back into the greenhouse. Disbud as necessary. Feed regularly until the buds show colour. Charm Chrysanthemums are raised from seed sown in spring — mounds of ferny foliage covered with scores of small daisy-like flowers

CINERARIA: The feature of this plant (Senecio cruentus) is a mass of daisy-like flowers covering the leaves in winter or early spring. Sow the seed in May. Many colours are available — the showiest strain is the Grandiflora group. The display should last for 4–7 weeks — throw the plants away after flowering

CLIVIA: Clusters of large orange flowers are borne in spring above the strap-like leaves. A rather temperamental plant — it does not like to be moved and it should not be re-potted unless the plant is pushing out of the container. Water sparingly between late autumn and early spring

COBAEA: The Cup and Saucer Vine is grown as an annual outdoors, but under glass it is a rampant perennial climber. Sow seed in early spring. The cup-shaped purple flowers appear in late summer — cut back the plants hard when flowering has finished

COLEUS: A plant grown for its colourful foliage rather than its insignificant flowers. Pinch out the tips to keep the plant bushy — cut back the stems and re-pot every spring. Sow seeds in early spring or take stem cuttings in spring or summer

CUPHEA: A 1 ft high bush which produces flowers from late spring to autumn. Red tubes with white and purple mouths — Cigar Plant is the common name. Sow seeds in spring or take cuttings in spring or summer. Cut back stems in early spring

Chrysanthemum morifolium Charm Pink

Clivia miniata

Coleus Salmon Lace

Senecio cruentus Exhibition Mixed

Greenhouse Pot Plants contd.

	Type grown
EXACUM: The flowers, pale purple with a gold centre, appear from midsummer to late autumn on this small and dainty plant. Sow in early spring and keep the compost moist at all times. Discard the plant after flowering	
FERNS: Many Ferns thrive in a cool greenhouse because of the moist summer air and the cool winter temperature. Summer shading is essential and so is the need to keep the compost moist at all times, but you cannot generalise too much about this group. Some require warm winter conditions and others must be kept at below 75°–80°F in summer. Choose one which is known to succeed in ordinary home greenhouses — included here are Adiantum, Cyrtomium, Nephrolepis and Pteris	
FOLIAGE HOUSE PLANTS: Only the hardiest house plants will survive over winter in a cold greenhouse, but numerous popular ones can be kept in the cool greenhouse. Examples are Asparagus Fern, Aspidistra, Chlorophytum, Fatshedera, Grevillea, Ivy, Norfolk Island Pine, Pilea and Tradescantia	
FUCHSIA: Most Fuchsias grown in the garden or as house plants are thrown away once the attractive pendant flowers have faded, but with a cool greenhouse these plants can be kept for several years. The rules are to cut back the stems and re-pot in early spring and to water sparingly in winter. Take cuttings in spring or summer — pinch the tips of young stems to induce bushiness. It takes about 8 weeks for plants to bloom after stopping. Stake or leave to trail — remove dead blooms to ensure regular bud formation	
GARDEN ANNUALS: A number of annuals sold for the garden rather than the greenhouse can be grown to provide a display under glass. Sow seed or buy as bedding plants in spring for a summer display — hardy annuals can be sown in autumn to flower in the spring. Successful types include Ageratum, Antirrhinum, Calendula, Clarkia, Convolvulus, Helichrysum, Godetia, Ipomoea, Larkspur, Lobelia, Nemesia, Nicotiana, Phlox, Stocks, Sweet Pea, Sweet Scabious, Tagetes, Viola and Zinnia	
GERBERA: The introduction of the Happipot strain has increased the popularity of this plant. Bright blooms on 1 ft stalks are produced instead of the lanky stems of the past. Sow seed in spring — grow in 5 in. pots. Overwinter at a minimum of 42°F — keep almost dry	
HELIOTROPE: Fragrant flower heads 4–6 in. across are produced in summer and autumn on this shrub. Sow seed in spring or take stem cuttings in summer — grow in a 5 in. pot. Keep the compost moist at all times during the growing season, but water sparingly in winter	
HIBISCUS: If you can maintain a minimum winter temperature of 50°F it should be possible to grow this superb shrub. The short-lived flowers appear in succession all summer long — 4–5 in. across and brightly coloured. Take stem cuttings in spring. Prune back stems in winter and water sparingly	
HOYA: An evergreen climber which bears clusters of starry flowers which are fragrant and either white or pale pink. H. carnosa can reach 15 ft so wires or trellis-work is needed. The flowering season is late spring to early autumn. Water very sparingly in winter and don't re-pot unless it is essential	
HYDRANGEA: This familiar garden shrub can be grown as a greenhouse plant — keep it in a large pot or tub. A cold greenhouse is ideal — warmth in winter is undesirable. Water copiously during the growing season — treat occasionally with MultiTonic. The familiar mop-heads appear in late spring and summer — in winter cut down stems which have flowered	
IMPATIENS: Most of the Busy Lizzies sold today are small and compact hybrids with flowers in white, orange, pink, purple and red. Even more exciting are the New Guinea types with multicoloured leaves. Seed can be sown in spring, although cuttings will root readily at almost any time of the year. Shade and water copiously during summer — dead-head regularly and cut back the stems by a half in winter	
JACOBINIA: A rare sight in the greenhouse, although the plume-like pink heads in late summer are attractive. Old plants are unproductive — either take cuttings in late spring or cut back the stems of old plants to a few inches above the compost	
JASMINE: Jasminum polyanthum is a vigorous climber for the cool house. The starry and fragrant white flowers open in winter. Cut back the ends of the stems after flowering and train the stems against a support. Keep the compost moist at all times — propagate in spring from stem cuttings	

Fuchsia Texas Longhorn

Hoya bella

Impatiens Zig-Zag

Pteris ensiformis victoriae

Greenhouse Pot Plants contd.

	Type grown

ORCHIDS: Some Orchids can survive quite happily at the winter temperatures expected in a cool greenhouse. Included here are Coelogyne, Cymbidium, Dendrobium, Odontoglossum, Laelia and Paphiopedilum. Shade and high air humidity are essential in summer — see The House Plant Expert (page 73)

PASSION FLOWER: Passiflora caerulea is a rampant climber which will outgrow its welcome if it is not cut back hard each year. The intricate flowers appear all summer long

PELARGONIUM: The well-known Geranium — the ever-popular Zonal types, the frilly large-flowered Regal ones and the trailing Ivy-leaved varieties. All sorts of flower and leaf colours are available, and a floral display can be obtained almost all year round if a minimum of 50°F is maintained. Pinch back young plants to induce bushiness. Re-pot only when it is essential. Provide plenty of fresh air and not much air humidity. Remove dead flowers and cut back all unnecessary stems in late autumn. Keep the compost almost dry if the minimum temperature in winter is in the 35°–45°F range

PLUMBAGO: Clusters of sky blue flowers appear throughout the summer and autumn on this rambling climber. Water sparingly in winter and cut back the stems at this stage. A minimum temperature of 45°F is required

POINSETTIA: A favourite winter house plant, but a rarity in lists of recommended greenhouse plants. Bought-in plants will make a fine display alongside the Chrysanthemums but a minimum temperature of 55°F is needed. Getting Poinsettia to bloom again is a tricky business

PRIMULA: P. malacoides is the most popular of the tender types which are grown. The fragrant small flowers are arranged in tiers on slender stalks. The flowers of P. obconica are large, fragrant and available in a wide range of colours, but the leaves can cause a rash on sensitive skins. Sow seeds in midsummer for flowering next spring. A minimum winter temperature of 45°F is needed. Polyanthus, low growing and large flowered, thrives in a cold house. Plant in the garden when the spring floral display is over

ROSE: Hybrid Tea bushes are planted in 7 in. pots in September. Leave the pots in the garden until December, then bring into the greenhouse. A minimum temperature of 45°F is required at this stage. Prune the stems hard in January — blooms appear in April. Harden off and stand the pot outdoors in May before re-potting in September

SAINTPAULIA: A favourite house plant, but not often recommended for the greenhouse. The reason is quite simple — the standard cool house is not warm enough to ensure their survival over winter — a minimum of 55°–60°F is needed. The best plan is to take the pots into the living room during the winter months. See The House Plant Expert (page 76) for details

SALPIGLOSSIS: An excellent plant for the greenhouse although it is not often recommended in the textbooks. Sow this half-hardy annual in early spring for summer flowering. The trumpet-shaped multicoloured flowers are 2 in. across

SCHIZANTHUS: Colourful, like Salpiglossis, and grown in the same way. The blooms are even more exotic — the common name is Poor Man's Orchid. Choose a compact variety such as Hit Parade

SOLANUM: S. capsicastrum (Winter Cherry) is a familiar sight at Christmas — the tiny flowers of summer turn to green berries in autumn and round red or orange balls in winter. Sow in early spring — stand outdoors during summer. Re-pot in spring. Take care — fruit is poisonous

STEPHANOTIS: A vigorous climber with stems reaching 10 ft or more. Take cuttings in May — not easy to root. The white waxy flowers appear in summer — the most outstanding feature is the intensity of the fragrance. A rather difficult plant which is prone to pest attack

STREPTOCARPUS: Many colourful hybrids have appeared in recent years, but Constant Nymph remains the favourite variety. A tricky plant — sow seed or take cuttings at re-potting time in spring. Flowers appear throughout the summer months. Needs winter warmth — minimum 50°F

STREPTOSOLEN: The Marmalade Bush is a rambling shrub which produces masses of orange blooms in late spring. A good one for the conservatory, but it tends to go leggy with age. Take stem cuttings in spring or summer — maintain a minimum of 45°–50°F in winter

THUNBERGIA: Black-eyed Susan is one of the best plants to choose for covering a large area quickly. Sow a few seeds of this annual climber in early spring for a succession of brown-throated flowers throughout the summer. Pinch out tips of young plants — keep the compost moist at all times

Passiflora caerulea

Pelargonium 'Carisbrooke'

Primula malacoides

Streptocarpus Constant Nymph

Bedding Plants

A bedding plant is generally an annual or occasionally a biennial or perennial which is raised under glass or in a nursery bed and then planted out in the garden as a temporary occupant to provide a colourful display. These seedlings are usually set out in large numbers as Groundwork Plants, but in some schemes individual tall plants with showy leaves or flowers are used as Dot Plants.

Most people buy their summer bedding plants as seedlings or rooted cuttings, but you can quite easily raise your own in a cool greenhouse. Begonias are raised from tubers — Pelargonium, Fuchsia, Dahlia, Heliotrope and Canna are propagated from cuttings. The rest are reproduced from seed. Growing your own means that you can choose from a vast selection of varieties — send off for a number of catalogues. Obviously you will save money if there are large areas to cover and you will also be able to ensure that the plants are in peak condition at transplanting time.

Sow in a heated propagator between late January and mid April. The hardier types and the slow growers are sown first — the late ones are quick growers and large-seeded types. Follow the rules set out on page 34 and harden off for 2-3 weeks before planting out in late May–early June.

Notes

Summer Bedding Plants

Latin name	Common name	Spacing	Height	Type grown
AGERATUM	Floss Flower	8 in.	8 in.	
ALYSSUM	Sweet Alyssum	9 in.	3–6 in.	
AMARANTHUS	Love-lies-bleeding	2 ft	3 ft	
ANTIRRHINUM	Snapdragon	9 in.–1½ ft	6 in.–3 ft	
BEGONIA	Tuberous Begonia	12–15 in.	1 ft	
BEGONIA	Wax Begonia	5–15 in.	6–9 in.	
CALCEOLARIA	Slipper Flower	9 in.	1 ft	
CALENDULA	Pot Marigold	1 ft	1–2 ft	
CALLISTEPHUS	China Aster	9 in.–1½ ft	9 in.–2½ ft	
CAMPANULA	Canterbury Bell	1 ft	1½–2½ ft	
CANNA	Indian Shot	2 ft	3 ft	
CELOSIA	Celosia	9 in.–1 ft	9 in.–2 ft	
CENTAUREA	Cornflower	9 in.–1 ft	1–2½ ft	
CHRYSANTHEMUM	Annual Chrysanthemum	1 ft	1½–2 ft	
COLEUS	Coleus	9–12 in.	1 ft	
CUPHEA	Firefly	12–15 in.	1 ft	
DAHLIA	Bedding Dahlia	1 ft	1–2 ft	
DIANTHUS	Annual Carnation	1 ft	1½ ft	

Ageratum houstonianum 'Blue Mink'

Callistephus chinensis

Chrysanthemum carinatum 'Court Jesters'

Summer Bedding Plants contd.

Latin name	Common name	Spacing	Height	Type grown
DIANTHUS	Indian Pink	6 in.	6 in.–1½ ft	
DIANTHUS	Sweet William	9 in.	1–2 ft	
FUCHSIA	Fuchsia	9 in.–3 ft	1–4 ft	
HELIOTROPIUM	Heliotrope	1–2 ft	1–3 ft	
IBERIS	Candytuft	9 in.	9 in.–1½ ft	
IMPATIENS	Busy Lizzie	6–9 in.	6 in.–1 ft	
KOCHIA	Kochia	1–2 ft	1–2 ft	
LOBELIA	Lobelia	6 in.	4–8 in.	
MATTHIOLA	Ten Week Stock	9 in.–1 ft	1–2½ ft	
NEMESIA	Nemesia	6 in.	9 in.–1½ ft	
NICOTIANA	Tobacco Plant	9 in.–1 ft	9 in.–3 ft	
PELARGONIUM	Regal Pelargonium	1 ft	1–2 ft	
PELARGONIUM	Zonal Pelargonium	1 ft	1–1½ ft	
PENSTEMON	Penstemon	1–1½ ft	1–2 ft	
PETUNIA	Petunia	6 in.–1 ft	6 in.–1½ ft	
PHLOX	Annual Phlox	8 in.	6 in.–1½ ft	
RICINUS	Castor-oil Plant	4 ft	4–5 ft	
SALVIA	Sage	1 ft	9 in.–1½ ft	
SCHIZANTHUS	Butterfly Flower	1 ft	1–1½ ft	
SENECIO	Cineraria	1–2½ ft	1–3 ft	
TAGETES	French Marigold	6–9 in.	6 in.–1 ft	
TAGETES	African Marigold	1–1½ ft	1–3 ft	
TAGETES	Tagetes	6–9 in.	6–9 in.	
VERBENA	Verbena	1 ft	6 in.–1 ft	
VIOLA	Pansy, Viola	9 in.–1 ft	6–9 in.	
ZEA	Ornamental Maize	4 ft	4–5 ft	
ZINNIA	Zinnia	6 in.–1 ft	6 in.–2½ ft	

Dianthus barbatus

Impatiens 'Grand Prix'

Lobelia erinus 'Mrs Clibran Improved'

Phlox drummondii

Zinnia 'Ruffles'

Garden Perennials and Shrubs

Your greenhouse should be more than an end in itself — not just a production unit for Tomatoes and Cucumbers and a display unit for pot plants. It should also serve as a supply point and a temporary refuge for many of the plants we grow in the house and garden.

Many owners put their greenhouses to this use for garden plants in the early part of the year. Bedding plants and vegetables are raised from seed for planting out once the danger of frost has passed, but for the rest of the year the greenhouse reverts to Tomatoes and pot plants. Described below are the ways the greenhouse can be used in the life of garden perennials and garden shrubs.

Chrysanthemums

In November lift the roots carefully and shake off the soil. Cut back the stems to about 4 in., trim off any leaves and label each plant. These prepared roots (stools) should be closely packed into boxes and surrounded by peat or compost. Place these boxes under the staging and keep them cool and fairly dry. Bring them into growth by increased watering in January and use the new shoots as cuttings during February or March. These cuttings should be 2–3 in. long and they should be taken from the base and not the sides of the stems. Root these cuttings at 50°–60°F and then transfer them to 3 in. pots. After hardening off plant out rooted cuttings in May — water pots thoroughly the day before.

Herbaceous Perennial propagation

The border plants grown in nearly all gardens are bought, provided by friends or derived from dividing clumps in spring. You can, however, raise most of them in the greenhouse, starting from seed, stem cuttings or root cuttings.

Seed sowing allows you to raise scores of plants which are not already in your garden. Use the technique described on page 34 — spring sowing should produce plants ready for putting into the border in the autumn. Some experts recommend sowing in early summer and then planting out in spring so that the first winter is spent protected under glass. Border perennials which can be raised from seed include Acanthus, Alstroemeria, Centranthus, Coreopsis, Delphinium, Dianthus, Gaillardia, Geum, Helianthus, Limonium, Linum, Lupin, Meconopsis, Platycodon, Primula and Salvia.

One of the problems of raising border plants from seed is that many named varieties cannot be propagated in this way. Cuttings are the answer — follow the rules laid down on page 35 and use The Flower Expert as your guide to timing. Young spring shoots, 2–3 in. tall, often make ideal cuttings.

Stem cuttings must be provided with some form of transparent cover to maintain a moist atmosphere — root cuttings are easier because they are simply planted in moist seed and cutting compost and left to produce shoots — just like planting a bulb. Use pieces of root 1–2 in. long. Insert into compost vertically and the right way up for half their length, then cover them completely with a layer of sharp sand. Water in and transplant into individual pots when new growth appears. Use for Anchusa, Centaurea, Phlox, Oriental Poppy, Gaillardia, Macleaya and Verbascum.

Dahlias

When the first frosts have blackened the foliage gently lift roots, taking care not to damage the tubers. Shake off excess soil and cut back the stems to about 6 in. — label and stand tubers upside down for a few days to drain off excess moisture. Place them on a layer of peat in deep boxes and cover the tubers (not the crowns) with more peat. Store the box under the staging until February, when it is time to start them into growth. Plant the roots in a damp peat/sand mix or in seed compost and place in a brightly-lit spot. Sever and trim the new shoots when they are about 3 in. high — use them as cuttings for potting up and then planting out in late May or early June when frost is no longer a danger.

For most people the Dahlia round consists of replanting the old tubers in mid April–mid May rather than using home-grown rooted cuttings. Only use tubers which have not been used for producing cuttings, and every couple of years divide up the tuber clumps carefully, making sure that each division has a piece of stem with swollen tubers attached. A better plan is to put the tuber clumps into a damp peat/sand mixture — in March or April stand the box or pots in a well-lit spot. When shoots have formed at the crown, cut each clump into planting pieces, each with at least one good-sized tuber and at least one stout shoot. Pot these up in Multicompost. Plant out as for rooted cuttings — see above.

Frost-sensitive Perennials and Shrubs

During September and October bring in tubs and pots of frost-sensitive plants which have stood in the garden to provide a display during the summer months. Included here are Citrus trees, Heliotrope, Agapanthus etc, but the most popular ones by far are Pelargonium and Fuchsia.

Pot up Pelargoniums which were bedded out during the summer — do this before the arrival of the first frosts. Any temperature between 33°–45°F will do, but you must keep the compost almost dry and ventilate whenever possible. Cut back top growth severely. The rules for overwintering Fuchsias are rather different — a minimum temperature of 42°–45°F is required and the compost should be kept slightly moist. In both cases the plants are brought back into growth in February by watering and placing them in a well-lit spot.

The time to place frost-sensitive plants outdoors depends on the district where you live. Between the end of May and the first 2 weeks of June is the usual time.

Shrub propagation

Many shrubs and trees can be propagated in the home greenhouse, but you will need patience. You will have to wait 1–4 years before the new plant is at the stage at which you can find it conveniently, if expensively, waiting for you at the local garden centre.

Do not begin from seed unless recommended to do so in the catalogue or textbook — some shrubs and trees take months to germinate or may need prolonged exposure to cold weather before they start to grow. Several shrubs can be readily raised from seed — examples include Cistus, Clerodendrum, Genista, Hippophae, Leycesteria and Potentilla. Sow in spring — follow the instructions on page 34.

The most important method of propagating shrubs is to strike semi-ripe stem cuttings in July or August. Sturdy side shoots are usually chosen, and the cutting should be soft and green at the top but somewhat woody and stiff at the base. The cuttings must be planted quickly and not left to dry out, and some form of glass or plastic cover will be required. Many popular garden shrubs can be propagated in this way. Taking cuttings of conifers is more difficult — tackle this job in September or October. Rooting will take 2–3 months.

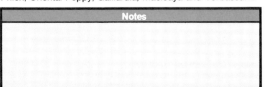

Notes

Tomatoes

In most greenhouses you will find Tomatoes growing on the south-facing side during the summer months. It is extremely satisfying to pick succulent fruit from June until October, and the flavour is outstanding if you have chosen the variety with care.

It is still a little surprising that we have an irrepressible urge to grow them. The plants need constant care — in summer it is necessary to water growing bags or pots every day. A wide range of pests and diseases find the Tomato an ideal host and so spraying is often necessary. Added to all these points is the fact that you can now buy really tasty varieties such as Gardener's Delight in the shops.

Perhaps the key is the fascination of watching tiny green pinheads swell into bright red fruits, plus the constant need we have in most households for both raw and cooked Tomatoes.

The standard greenhouse varieties are Cordon (single-stemmed) plants which require support — they will grow 6 ft or more if not stopped. It is unfortunate that most gardeners refuse to be adventurous — each year they plant Alicante, Ailsa Craig or Moneymaker, but there are so many exciting new varieties to try. There are the giant Beefsteaks at one end of the scale and the small and sweet Cherry Tomatoes at the other. Where height is a problem grow a Bush type instead of a Cordon — little or no training, de-shooting or stopping is required, although growth is rather untidy.

Growing methods

- Tomatoes can be grown in **border soil** — raised beds are more satisfactory than beds at ground level. Prepare the soil in winter — dig in peat and a small amount of compost or well-rotted manure. Rake in Growmore fertilizer shortly before planting. Do not plant too early — the soil temperature should be at least 55°F or growth will be checked. A good method in new soil if you can't tend to plants every day, but the border soon becomes infested with soil pests and root diseases. This means that it must either be sterilised or changed after a couple of seasons.

- **Ring culture** overcomes this difficulty and gives high yields, but it has never become a popular technique. A 6 in. deep trench is lined with plastic sheeting and filled with fine gravel. Bottomless pots (9 or 10 in.) are filled with potting compost into which the Tomato seedlings are planted. The pots are set along the gravel layer at 24 in. intervals. The gravel base is kept watered — liquid feeds are applied at weekly intervals to the pots ('rings').

- **Pot culture** is straightforward, but yields tend to be moderate. Watering at least once a day will be necessary in summer. Use 10 or 12 in. pots and stand about 24 in. apart.

- **Growing bags** have become by far the most popular Tomato growing method with both the professional nurseryman and amateur gardener. Plant 2, 3 or 4 seedlings, according to the manufacturer's instructions. An excellent and reliable method .... if you master the watering technique.

Sowing

- If you need a large number of plants, then follow the conventional technique of sowing thinly in trays or pans filled with seed compost or Multicompost — see page 34 for details. Cover lightly with compost — keep moist but not wet at 60°-65°F. Germination will take place in about 5-7 days. When the seedlings have formed a pair of true leaves prick them out into 3 in. peat pots filled with potting compost.

- If only a few plants are required, it is easier to sow a couple of seeds in 3 in. peat pots of compost, removing the weaker seedling after germination. Sow up a few more pots than you will actually need — 'rogue' seedlings showing abnormal growth will have to be discarded.

Planting

- Plant seedlings when they are 6-8 in. tall and the flowers of the first truss are beginning to open. Choose shop-bought seedlings with care — avoid lanky stems, yellow or distorted leaves and any sign of abnormal growth. Water the pots thoroughly before planting out into growing bags, border soil or large pots. Plant 18-24 in. apart in the border.

Types

ORDINARY varieties (O)
This group of red salad Tomatoes contains several old favourites which are grown for reliability (Moneymaker), flavour (Ailsa Craig) or earliness (Harbinger).

F₁ HYBRID varieties (F₁)

F_1 HYBRID varieties (F_1)
This group bears fruit which is similar in appearance to the Ordinary varieties, but these modern crosses have two important advantages — they are generally heavier yielding and also have a high degree of disease resistance.

BEEFSTEAK varieties (B)
This group produces the large and meaty Tomatoes which are so popular in the U.S and on the Continent. They are excellent for sandwiches but only you can decide whether their flavour is superior to our familiar salad varieties. There are three types — the true 'beefsteak' hybrids such as Dombello, the giant hybrids such as Big Boy, and the non-hybrid Marmandes which are suitable only for outdoor growing. Stop the plants when the fourth truss has set and provide support for the fruit if necessary.

NOVELTY varieties (N)
Catalogues sing the praises of the yellow and striped varieties but they remain distinctly unpopular. The first Tomatoes sent to Europe were gold-coloured and not red, but that was a long time ago.

Varieties

Varieties	Type	Variety grown
AILSA CRAIG: The best-flavoured variety in the Ordinary group. Fruits are medium-sized and brightly coloured. Listed in most catalogues	O	
ALICANTE: Moneymaker type — heavy cropping and reliable. There are advantages — resistant to greenback and the flavour is good. Very popular	O	
BIG BOY: The most popular of the giant Tomatoes — fruits weigh 1 lb or more. For maximum size disbud to 3 fruits per truss	B	
CURABEL: The variety from which Shirley was selected — usually sold by suppliers who don't stock Shirley. Both are quite similar	F_1	
DOMBELLO: A super-giant, according to the suppliers. Central core is absent and the flavour is good. Recommended for cold houses	B	
EUROCROSS A: A popular choice for a heated greenhouse — large fruits on leaf mould-resistant and greenback-immune plants. Good flavour	F_1	
GARDENER'S DELIGHT: Bite-sized Tomatoes with a superb tangy flavour. Trusses are long and heavy. This old favourite can be grown outdoors or under glass	O	
GOLDEN BOY: This variety is basically a Beefsteak Tomato, but the skin is yellow. The fruits are very large and the texture is meaty	N	
GOLDEN SUNRISE: The usual choice for the gardener who wants a yellow Tomato. The fruits are medium-sized with a distinctive taste	N	
HARBINGER: The earliest of the Ordinary varieties listed here. There are no other outstanding virtues, but flavour is good	O	
HERALD: A vigorous and early-cropping variety. Tops for sweetness and flavour, according to some experts. Fruits are medium-sized	F_1	
IDA: An early and heavy-cropping variety which is recommended for cold houses. Disease resistance is good — fruits are medium-sized	F_1	
MONEYMAKER: Still popular, but newer varieties are taking over. Trusses are large but the flavour is bland. Fruits are medium-sized	O	
ODINE: An excellent choice for a small greenhouse — growth is compact but yields are high. An early cropper with outstanding resistance to disease	F_1	
RED ALERT: A recent introduction which has become popular. Very early, bearing small fruits with an excellent flavour. A compact Bush variety	O	
SHIRLEY: Few varieties can rival this one. Heavy yields, early crops, good disease resistance and unaffected by short cold spells	F_1	
SWEET 100: Another outdoor/greenhouse variety — over a hundred cherry-sized fruits can be picked from one plant. Flavour is excellent	F_1	
TIGERELLA: An oddity — the fruits bear tiger stripes of red and yellow when mature. The yields are good and so is the flavour	N	
TORNADO: The best Bush Tomato for growing in the greenhouse. Compact and early — the foliage is sparse but crops are heavy	F_1	

Alicante

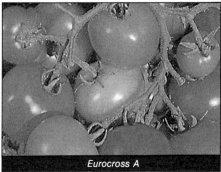
Eurocross A

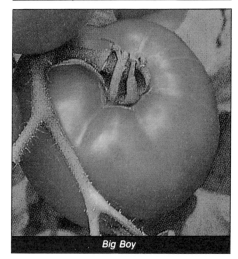
Big Boy

Gardener's Delight

Caring for the Crop

● Tie the stem loosely to a stout cane or wind it clockwise up a well-anchored but slack length of rough twine. Be careful not to damage the stem during this operation — you will find it easier to turn the string around the plant.

● Side shoots will appear where the leaf stalks join the stem. De-shooting is necessary — this calls for snapping them off when they are about 1 in. long. Do this job cleanly — do not leave broken stumps. You will find it easier to achieve this at the start of the day rather than in the afternoon.

● Water regularly to keep the soil constantly moist at all times. Too little or too infrequently will result in poor and damaged fruit — too much or too frequently will result in rotten roots and stems. Be guided by the conditions and the growth stage — a plant in full fruit may need watering 2 or 3 times a day in midsummer.

● Feeding can begin when the first fruits have set and should be continued according to the maker's instructions until the last truss has set. Use a liquid and not a powder or granular fertilizer — make sure that it contains magnesium.

● Remove the leaves below the first truss when the plants are about 4 ft high. This de-leafing process below fruit trusses can be continued as the season progresses, but only if the leaves are yellow, damaged or diseased. Never overdo this de-leafing operation. Use a sharp knife to remove the unwanted foliage.

● Mist the flowers at midday and tap the supports occasionally to aid pollen dispersion and fruit set.

● Try to avoid wide fluctuations in temperature — aim to keep the maximum below 80°F. Ventilation is essential in summer — open up when the temperature exceeds 70°F. Shade by painting the outside with Coolglass in order to keep down the temperature and to protect the fruit from scorch and other problems.

● Remove the tip at 2 leaves above the top truss once the plant has reached the top of the house or when 7 trusses have set.

Harvesting

● Pick the fruit when they are ripe and fully coloured. Hold the Tomato in your palm and with your thumb break off the fruit at the knuckle (swelling on the flower stalk). Do not leave fruit on the plant after they are fully ripe — flavour declines with age.

● Finish picking between late September and mid October, depending on the season and locality. Unripe fruit should be placed as a layer in a tray which is then put in a drawer. Next to the tray set a couple of ripe Apples which will generate the fruit-ripening gas ethylene.

Problems

Diseases and disorders are much more important than insect pests; although whitefly, red spider mite and aphid may be troublesome.

Problems due to poor ventilation

Tomato leaf mould   **Botrytis**

Mildews and moulds flourish in damp, cool air — the diseases illustrated above are a sure sign that ventilation is inadequate. Remove diseased portions — spray with carbendazim.

Problems due to poor watering practice

Split fruit   **Foot rot**

Poor drainage and waterlogging result in foot rot and root rot, especially with plants in border soil. Heavy watering following dryness at the roots leads to split fruit (above) or blossom end rot (page 38).

Problems due to overheating or too much sun

Sun scald   **Greenback**

Blotchy ripening (page 38), sun scald and greenback are signs of too much heat and too much sun.

Problems due to dry air

Blossom drop   **Dry set**

Blossom drop and fruit drop (dry set) are caused by imperfect pollination. Dry air is a common cause. Mist the open flowers and tiny fruit — damp down regularly.

Calendar

In a heated greenhouse kept at a minimum night temperature of 50°-55°F Tomato seed is sown in late December and planted out in late February or early March for a May–June crop.

Most gardeners, however, grow Tomatoes in an unheated ('cold') house. Sow seed in early March and plant out in late April or early May. The first fruit will be ready for picking in July.

	JAN	FEB	MAR	APR	MAY	JUN	JUL	AUG	SEP	OCT	NOV	DEC
Recommended Sowing Time (heated greenhouse)	sow	plant	plant									sow
Actual Sowing Dates (heated greenhouse)												
Recommended Sowing Time (cold greenhouse)		sow	sow	plant	plant							
Actual Sowing Dates (cold greenhouse)												
Expected Picking Time							heated	cold	cold	cold		
Actual Picking Dates												

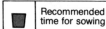 Recommended time for sowing

 Recommended time for planting

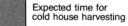 Expected time for cold house harvesting

Expected time for start of heated house harvesting

Cucumbers

A well-grown specimen of a greenhouse Cucumber, straight and cylindrical, smooth-skinned and glistening, may reach 18 in. or more in length. A thing of beauty perhaps, but until recently it was customary for textbooks to warn the reader about the difficulties. The so-called Ordinary varieties (see below) need a moister atmosphere than Tomatoes and the side shoots have to be trained along horizontal wires. Male flowers have to be removed and both pests and diseases are often a headache.

The introduction of the All-female varieties has changed the situation quite dramatically. These F_1 hybrids are as easy to grow as Tomatoes, and sometimes even easier. The fruit is borne on the axils of the leaves and main stem and not on side shoots, so training up a single support is all that is needed. Male flowers rarely if ever appear, and disease is much less of a problem.

Outdoor varieties have improved greatly during the past few years and one is tempted these days to grow this crop in the garden rather than under glass. However if you want to pick Cucumbers in June or July for midsummer salads then growing them in the greenhouse is the only answer.

Sowing

- Cucumber seed germinates quickly, but warmth (65°–70°F) is essential. Place a single seed edge-ways ½ in. deep in seed compost or Multicompost in a 3 in. peat pot. This should be timed for about 4 weeks before planting.

- Germination takes place in 2–3 days — do not use seedlings which germinate after this time. Keep the compost moist. Do not allow the seedlings to become pot-bound — transfer to 5 in. pots if necessary.

Planting

- Plant seedlings when they are 8–10 in. tall and there are 2 well-formed true leaves. Choose shop-bought seedlings with care — they should be a rich green colour and the variety should be stated. Water the pots thoroughly before planting — one in a 12–15 in. pot or 2 per growing bag.

- Planting in border soil is not recommended as soil sickness soon becomes a problem. If you do decide to go ahead then plant on the top of a ridge of soil, spacing the plants 2 ft apart.

Caring for the Crop

- The temperature after planting out should be no lower than 60°–65°F.

- Keep the compost thoroughly moist at all times, but do be careful not to keep the compost soggy for the first 2 or 3 weeks after planting out. Little and often is the watering rule, and avoid waterlogging at all costs.

- Adequate ventilation will be necessary, and so will regular damping down. Hose down the floor, but not the plants, to maintain the humidity of the air.

- With Ordinary varieties it is necessary to run a series of horizontal training wires 12 in. apart up the wall and across the roof. The fruit-bearing side shoots are tied along these wires. Pinch out the growing point when the main shoot reaches the ridge. The tip of each side shoot is pinched out at 2 leaves beyond a female flower. Female flowers have a miniature Cucumber behind them — male flowers have just a thin stalk. Remember to remove all male flowers promptly — fertilized fruit is bitter. Pinch out tips of flowerless side shoots when they reach 2 ft in length.

- Things are much simpler with All-female varieties. Horizontal training wires are not needed — merely train the stem up a stout cane or vertical wire. Twist the stem around the wire or cane every few days. Fruits are borne on the main stem, so remove all side shoots. Do take care, however, not to remove the tiny fruits at the same time. Remove all flowers from the bottom 2 ft of the stem.

- Feed every 2 weeks with a Tomato Fertilizer once the first fruits have started to swell.

- Apply Coolglass to protect the fruit from the glare of midsummer sun.

Harvesting

- Cut (do not pull) when the fruit has reached a reasonable size and the sides are parallel. Use secateurs or a sharp knife. Pick regularly — cropping will cease if you allow Cucumbers to mature and turn yellow on the plant.

Problems

- A whole host of pests and diseases can attack Cucumbers under glass, but not many are likely to trouble you. Whitefly, aphid and red spider mite will usually appear, and so will powdery mildew if the compost is dry and the air is moist. Keeping the compost too wet leads to root rot or botrytis.

- Bitter fruit is perhaps the most common problem. A sudden drop in temperature or soil moisture can cause this trouble — so can a sudden increase in sunshine or de-shooting. The most usual cause is pollination — remember to remove male flowers promptly. Better still, grow an All-female variety.

Types

ORDINARY varieties (O)
The traditional Cucumber for the exhibitor — long, straight and smooth. But these varieties are generally demanding — warm and moist air is necessary and so is training of the side shoots along horizontal wires.

ALL-FEMALE varieties (A-F)
These modern F_1 hybrids have several advantages. The tiresome job of removing male flowers is not required and the plants are much more resistant to disease. They are also easier to grow and require only a simple cane for support.

Varieties

Varieties	Type	Variety grown
AMSLIC: A good choice for the cold greenhouse — you can even grow this one outdoors. Yields are high and mildew resistance is outstanding	A-F	
BUTCHER'S DISEASE RESISTING: Another old favourite like Telegraph — rougher-skinned but higher-yielding than its rival. You can do better these days	O	
CRYSTAL APPLE: An odd one indeed — small, round and yellow with outstanding flavour and juiciness. Easy to grow alongside Tomatoes or pot plants	O	
FEMBABY: The baby of the group, small enough to grow on a windowsill. The compact plants are easy to train — fruit is about half normal size	A-F	
FEMSPOT: The most handsome of the modern F_1 hybrids, but you will only get the exhibition-quality fruits if you provide enough warmth and moisture	A-F	
KOSURA: An excellent choice for the North — good quality fruit can be obtained in a cold house even in cool districts	A-F	
KYOTO: An example of the Japanese Group. The outstanding feature is the ease of growth — even easier than growing Tomatoes. Fruit is long and straight	O	
MONIQUE: Good quality fruit is produced under Tomato house conditions — the number and weight of the crop is outstanding. Easy to grow	A-F	
PEPINEX 69: The first of the All-females, formerly known as Femina. A good example of the group, but it needs warmer conditions than some newer ones	A-F	
PETITA: The fruits are only about 8 in. long but a large number are borne. It grows well under cool conditions but some male flowers are produced	A-F	
SIGMADEW: Suitable for the cold house. This one is something of a novelty — it is thin-skinned, fine-flavoured and almost white	O	
TELEGRAPH: An old variety named when the telegraph was a new invention. Despite its age and limitations, Telegraph is still popular	O	
TOPSY: Tops for flavour, according to the experts. Yields, however, are not very good and the seeds are not widely available	A-F	
UNIFLORA D: The self-pruning Cucumber. Side shoots grow about 6 in. long and then stop — no pinching out is needed. A high-yielding variety	A-F	

Femspot

Telegraph

Crystal Apple

Calendar

In a heated greenhouse kept at a minimum night temperature of 55°F, Cucumber seed is sown in early March and planted out in April for a May-June crop.

Most gardeners, however, grow Cucumbers in an unheated ('cold') house. Sow seed in late April and plant out in late May. The first fruit will be ready for picking in July.

	JAN	FEB	MAR	APR	MAY	JUN	JUL	AUG	SEP	OCT	NOV	DEC
Recommended Sowing Time (heated greenhouse)			🪣	🏠								
Actual Sowing Dates (heated greenhouse)												
Recommended Sowing Time (cold greenhouse)				🪣	🏠							
Actual Sowing Dates (cold greenhouse)												
Expected Picking Time												
Actual Picking Dates												

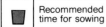 Recommended time for sowing

 Recommended time for planting

Expected time for cold house harvesting

Expected time for start and end of heated house harvesting

Vegetables

The usual reason for growing greenhouse vegetables is the ability to grow tender plants which are unpredictable outdoors or even impossible in some districts — Aubergines, Capsicums, Tomatoes etc. In addition there is the satisfaction of harvesting produce before the outdoor crop is ready — early Potatoes, early Carrots and so on. But there is an additional advantage which is just as important but does not appear in the standard textbooks — the ability to care for your plants without having to worry about weather, wind or weeds.

The greenhouse has another role to play in the cultivation of vegetables. It can be used to give garden-grown varieties an early start in life by sowing them in a propagator, pricking out into trays or pots and then planting them outdoors in order to gain several weeks' advantage over garden-sown specimens.

Greenhouse Vegetables

The greenhouse is their permanent home, from seed sowing to harvest. Some types are too tender to be trusted outdoors, others are half-hardy and need the extended growing season provided by greenhouse cultivation. Others are varieties of hardy vegetables which produce an early crop when grown under glass. One basic rule — make sure that the variety selected is recommended for greenhouse cultivation.

Garden Vegetables

The greenhouse is their nursery, from seed sowing to planting outdoors. Hardy varieties are sown from January or February onwards and planted out when the soil is suitable. Half-hardy vegetables are sown about 6–8 weeks before the expected planting time.

Greenhouse Vegetables

	Type grown
AUBERGINE: The Aubergine or Egg Plant is one of the new wave of vegetables which were once regarded as unusual but are now available from greengrocers and supermarkets everywhere. It can be grown as easily as the Tomato. Sow seeds in compost-filled peat pots in late February — keep at 60°–65°F. Plant 3 to a growing bag — remove the growing point when the plant is 12 in. high and stake stems. When 5 fruits have formed, remove lateral shoots and remaining flowers. Mist regularly. Cut fruit when it is 5–6 in. long and still shiny. Recommended varieties: Long Purple, Black Prince	
BEETROOT: A catch crop to grow between tall vegetables in border soil. The seeds are sown directly in the soil in February or March between the planting sites planned for Tomatoes or Cucumbers. Thin to 4 in. apart — pull in late May or June whilst the roots are still small. Recommended varieties: Boltardy, Arran Early, Early Bunch	
CAPSICUM: The large Sweet Pepper is becoming increasingly popular — it requires similar conditions to the Tomato. Sow seeds in compost-filled peat pots in late February — keep at 60°–65°F. Plant 3 or 4 to a growing bag. Mist plants regularly to keep down red spider mite and to encourage fruit set. Some form of support is necessary — pinching out the growing point is not recommended. Water regularly — feed with Bio Tomato Food once fruit has started to swell. Pick when green or red, swollen and glossy. Recommended varieties: Canape, New Ace, Gypsy	
CARROT: A useful catch crop. Sow between January and March for a May crop or in September for December pulling. Sow very thinly in drills 9 in. apart. Thin out the seedlings when they are large enough to handle — leave the seedlings 2 in. apart. Pull as required. Recommended varieties: Short-rooted varieties only — Amsterdam Forcing, Tiana, Early Nantes, Amstel	
COURGETTE: Be warned — this crop takes up a lot of floor space. Sow seeds in compost-filled peat pots in April — one seed per pot edgeways ½ in. below the surface. Keep at 65°–70°F. When 6 in. high plant into growing bags — 2 per bag. Keep well watered — hand pollinate the flowers with a soft brush or cotton wool ball. Feed once fruit has started to swell — cut when 4–5 in. long. Recommended varieties: Zucchini, Golden Zucchini	
CUCUMBER: See pages 21–22	
FRENCH BEAN: Both climbing and bush French Beans can be grown under glass to provide a May or June crop. Sow the seeds between January and March in compost-filled peat pots — keep at 60°–65°F. Transplant into pots (5 in an 8 in. pot) or into growing bags (6–8 per bag). A pod is ready for picking when it snaps easily when bent — pick several times a week if necessary. Recommended varieties: Masterpiece, Tendergreen, Blue Lake, Garrafal Oro	

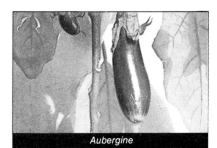
Aubergine

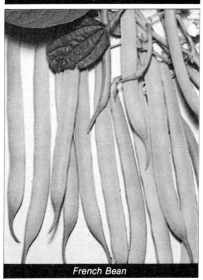
Capsicum

French Bean

Greenhouse Vegetables contd.

	Type grown

HERBS: Many herbs die down in the open garden when late autumn arrives. It is therefore a good plan to dig and pot up clumps of Chives, Parsley, Mint, Rosemary, Sage and Thyme. Keep the pots watered — remove dead or dying leaves promptly. Sow herb seeds in March

Lettuce

LETTUCE: A good use for growing bags after Tomatoes or Cucumbers have been lifted — plant 2 rows of 6 seedlings in each bag. Sow seed at 55°–60°F (not higher) — the correct time for sowing depends on the variety, and do make sure the variety is recommended for glasshouse growing. Late summer-sown ones for winter cropping include Kwiek and Marmer. Winter-sown ones for spring cropping include Emerald and Sea Queen. Kloek can be sown in autumn in a cold house for harvesting in spring. Lettuce for summer harvesting is generally grown outdoors, but you can sow May Queen in spring for June-August cropping. Do not overwater — keep watch for slugs and botrytis

MUSHROOM: These days you are spared the need to prepare your own compost and then impregnate it with spawn — you can buy a ready-to-grow plastic-bucket kit. Simply follow the instructions — an expensive way to grow Mushrooms but it is no bother. Buttons should appear after about a month — harvest by gently pulling and twisting — fill the hole with the compost after removal

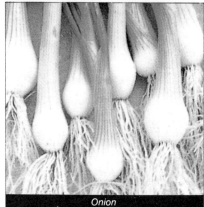
Onion

MUSTARD & CRESS: The old favourite for salads, garnishing and sandwiches — useful greenstuff to grow all year round. Place several sheets of kitchen paper towelling at the bottom of a shallow plastic tray. Dampen thoroughly and pour off excess water. Sow Cress evenly and thickly — 3 days later sow Mustard over the emerging Cress seedlings. Keep constantly moist — harvest in about 14 days when seedlings are 2 in. high

ONION: Another use for old growing bags. Grow Spring Onions by sprinkling seed thinly along rows — sow in September for an April crop or in February for pulling in June. Space rows 6–8 in. apart — use the thinnings for cooking and the fully-formed plants for salads. Recommended variety: White Lisbon

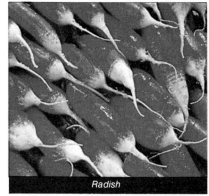
Radish

POTATO: Early Potatoes are easy to grow in a cold greenhouse — plant sprouted seed Potatoes in January for a May crop or in August for harvesting on Christmas day. Plant in a 10 in. pot (1 per pot) or in a growing bag (2 per bag). Harvest by gathering the required number of Potatoes from the top part of the container — repeat several times before lifting the plant. Recommended varieties: Epicure, Maris Bard, Pentland Javelin, Sutton's Foremost

RADISH: A useful vegetable for growing between other plants or in odd corners at almost any time of the year, although the most popular times for sowing are between February and May and again in the autumn. This crop is quick growing and takes up little room — sowing to harvest may take as little as 3 weeks. Sow ½ in. deep in rows 6 in. apart — sow thinly and no thinning should be required. Recommended varieties: Cherry Belle, Saxerre, Large White Icicle

TOMATO: See pages 18–20

TURNIP: Not often mentioned in books on greenhouse growing, but a good crop for the border before planting up Tomatoes or for using old growing bags. Sow ½ in. deep in rows 6 in. apart — thin to leave seedlings 4 in. apart. Sow in February for pulling in May — harvest the roots while they are still small — no larger than an egg. Recommended varieties: Early varieties only — Jersey Navet, Snowball, Tokyo Cross

Turnip

Garden Vegetables

All sorts of vegetables can be started off in the greenhouse to give them an early start in the garden. Seed is germinated in a heated propagator or in an airing cupboard if a propagator is not available. The seedlings are then grown on in the greenhouse until the time for planting outdoors arrives. Basic rules include sowing thinly, pricking out promptly and hardening off thoroughly.

Follow the rules set out on page 34. Use trays for small seeds and then prick out into trays filled with Multicompost — a better alternative is to transplant the seedlings into peat blocks or small peat pots which avoid root disturbance at planting time. Large seeds are spaced out about 2 in. apart in trays or they can be sown into pots.

If possible cover the soil with cloches for 2 weeks before planting and for some time after planting. This will get the crop off to a flying start.

Vegetable	When to sow	When to plant	Type grown
AUBERGINE	March–April	B	
BEAN, BROAD	February–March	A	
BEAN, FRENCH	April	B	
BEAN, RUNNER	April	B	
BEETROOT	February–March	A	
BROCCOLI	April	A	
BRUSSELS SPROUT	February–March	A	
CABBAGE, SPRING	July–August	A	
CABBAGE, SUMMER	February–March	A	
CABBAGE, WINTER	April	A	
CABBAGE, SAVOY	April	A	
CAPSICUM	April	B	
CARROT	February	A	
CAULIFLOWER	January–March	A	
CELERIAC	March	B	
CELERY	April	B	
CHICORY	April	A	
COURGETTE	April	B	
CUCUMBER	April	B	
ENDIVE	January–July	A	
KOHL RABI	February	A	
LEEK	February–March	A	
LETTUCE	January–July	A	
MARROW	April	B	
ONION	February–March	A	
PARSNIP	February	A	
PEA	February–May	A	
SALSIFY	March	A	
SPINACH	February	A	
SWEDE	March	A	
SWEET CORN	April	B	
TOMATO	March–April	B	
TURNIP	February	A	

A	Plant about 4–6 weeks after sowing. The essential requirement is good soil conditions — neither dry nor wringing wet. Seedlings are ready for planting when roots start to peep out at the bottom of the seed tray
B	Plant when the danger of frost has passed. This depends on the location — from mid May in favoured districts in the South and West to the second week in June for unfavourable areas in the North

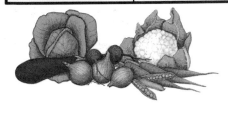

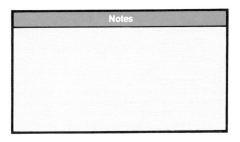

Notes

FORCING

The use of the greenhouse for the vegetables described on the left is to give them a good start in life. The use of the greenhouse for forcing is at the other end of the time scale — forcing involves bringing mature plants inside the house for the final stage before cropping.

RHUBARB

Dig up the crowns in November and leave them exposed to frost on the surface of the soil. After this has taken place, pack the roots closely together in a deep box, filling up the spaces in between with old compost or peat. Leave the crowns exposed. Cover the box with black polythene and place it under the staging. In about 4 weeks you will be able to pick tender sticks — harvest them as soon as they are large enough to use. When harvesting is over dispose of the crowns as they are of no further use.

CHICORY

The first stage is to lift the roots in November — discard fanged ones and roots less than 1 in. across at the crown. Cut off the tops about 1 in. above the crown and cut back roots to 6 in. Pack them horizontally in a box of sand in a cool shed. Force a few of these roots at a time between November and March — do this by planting 5 in a 9 in. pot and surrounding them with damp peat or compost. Leave the crowns exposed and cover with an empty pot in which the drainage hole has been blocked. Plump leafy heads (chicons) will form. Cut them when they are about 6 in. high — this will take about 3–4 weeks.

Fruit

A cool house should be a home for fruit as well as vegetables and pot plants. Unfortunately Peaches and Grapes have given fruit a bad image for the owner of a small structure — these vigorous plants are excellent against the wall of a large lean-to but have no place in an 8 ft x 6 ft greenhouse. Even here, however, there is the place for some fruit — a few pots of Strawberries for picking in April and a growing bag with Melons to produce fruits in July.

The length of time that the plant resides in the house depends on the type. Apricot and Nectarine are permanent residents which stay for many years. Others such as Melon live there for their whole lives, but this only lasts from spring to autumn. Strawberries are temporary residents, staying for only a few months in the greenhouse where they bear fruit. The least permanent of the residents are hardy fruit trees in pots which are brought in for only a few weeks around blossom time.

	Notes

	Type grown
APRICOT: This fruit is notoriously unreliable outdoors in the South and quite unsuitable for the North. It does well in a greenhouse as the blossom is protected from frost in early spring and fruit ripening is enhanced at the end of the season. High temperatures are not needed and are a definite disadvantage in winter — during the dormant season the plants need fresh air and temperatures which get down to 35°F or even less. The best way to grow an Apricot is in the form of a fan planted against the wall of a large lean-to. The structure should ideally face South — don't bother with Apricots if it faces North. Apricots are self-fertile, so only one plant is needed. Planting time is between November and January — prepare the border soil in October. Buy a 2 or 3 year old partly-trained tree — see The Fruit Expert for details of training and maintenance pruning. During the growing season water regularly and feed occasionally. Make sure the house is well-ventilated at flowering time. Hand pollinate and thin fruit to 4–6 in. apart. Harvest in August when the fruit comes away easily from the tree. It is possible to grow Apricots in pots or large tubs but the container becomes too small after a few years and both growth and yields decline.	
CAPE GOOSEBERRY: A rarity in the shops but you will find it in many seed catalogues. Grow it as a half-hardy annual — the cultural needs are the same as Tomatoes. Take care, however — it is a vigorous and leafy plant which is out of place in a small greenhouse. Pinch out the growing points when 1 ft high to induce bushiness — tie the stems loosely to 4 ft stakes. Protect from whitefly and leave the fruits to ripen on the plants in late summer — golden shiny balls within brown and papery husks.	
FIG: Don't plant a Fig in the border soil — it will turn into a large leafy jungle which bears little fruit. Grow it in a large pot or tub. Train it as a fan against the wall or as a dwarf bush — even a 4 ft bush will produce a worthwhile crop. Buy a 2 or 3 year old partly-trained tree. See The Fruit Expert for instructions on training and maintenance pruning. Figs are a demanding crop — fruit thinning is quite complicated and daily watering will be necessary in summer. Re-pot every 2 years and feed when fruit have formed. Little attention, however, is needed when the leaves fall — stop watering and keep the compost dry over winter.	
GRAPE: There is no escaping the fact that Grapes are a time-consuming crop. For the enthusiast there is stem cleaning in midwinter, spring and summer pruning, regular watering all summer long, fruit thinning in autumn and pruning of the leading shoots in early winter. All these tasks are described in The Fruit Expert, but you might like to try the following simplified routine. Yields will not be high and you will have to start again after about 4 years, but little work is involved. Plant a 2 or 3 year old Black Hamburgh in a 12 in. pot in December. Put the pot outdoors and bring back in February. Push three 5 ft canes into the compost near the rim — tie the top ends together to form a wigwam. Train the stems spirally around the canes. Stop lateral branches at 2 leaves beyond each bunch of Grapes — thin these down to leave just 6 bunches per plant. In winter cut back the main stems (rods) to half their length.	

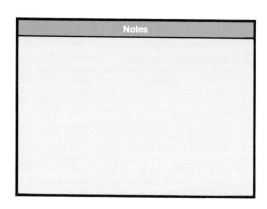
Apricot

Cape Gooseberry

Grape

Fruit contd.

	Type grown

HARDY FRUIT IN POTS: The introduction of dwarfing root-stocks has made the cultivation of hardy tree fruit such as Apples and Pears a practical proposition. The trees are planted in a 12–15 in. container and are moved indoors in winter and at blossom time — hand pollination is necessary. Remember that Apples and Pears are generally not self-fertile — choose a 'family tree' bearing several varieties. After petal fall the pot is stood outdoors on the terrace or in the garden. Watering every day will be necessary in a dry summer.

Peach

KIWI FRUIT: Once a rarity, now seen in shops everywhere. You will sometimes see this fruit recommended as a greenhouse crop, but it really is not a good idea. Kiwi Fruit is a vigorous climber with very large leaves — the dense shade would create all sorts of problems for you.

MELON: If you can grow Cucumbers well then you should succeed with Melons. Raise the plants in exactly the same way and plant the seedlings in growing bags — 2 per bag. A cane will be necessary behind each plant and there should be horizontal support wires 1 ft apart. The lateral branches are trained along these wires — nip off their tips when 5 leaves have been produced.

Hand pollination of the female flowers is essential. Stop the stems 2 leaves beyond the developing fruit and reduce the number to leave 4–6 Melons per plant. Support each one with a net, and pick when the end away from the stalk gives slightly when gently pressed. The experts agree — choose Sweetheart.

Kiwi Fruit

NECTARINE: Nectarine is a smooth-skinned sport of Peach. It is cultivated in the same way, although yields are lower and it has a rather more delicate constitution.

PEACH: Like the Apricot this fruit tree benefits from the protection and warmth of a greenhouse both at blossom time and fruit-ripening time. The wall of a south-facing lean-to is the traditional place for a Peach tree, but you can grow a bush in a 12 in. pot. Buy a 2 or 3 year old partly-trained tree — see The Fruit Expert for details of training and maintenance pruning. High humidity is necessary during the growing season — damp down regularly. Regular watering is also necessary — in summer that may mean once or even twice a day. Hand pollinate and thin fruit to 6–9 in. apart.

Harvest when the flesh around the stalk is soft and the skin bears a reddish flush. During the autumn and winter keep the house cool and open up the ventilators. Don't worry if winter temperatures fall to freezing point.

Melon

STRAWBERRY: Here is a fruit which every greenhouse owner can grow, however small the house. In August or September plant vigorous and well-rooted plants into 6 in. pots. Water regularly and bury the pots outside in well-drained ground or peat in November to protect the roots from frost.

In January bring the pots into a cool greenhouse — keep them in a well-lit spot. When the flowers open stop damping down and hand pollinate the blooms and start to feed weekly with a liquid fertilizer. Ventilate the house when the weather is warm and sunny. Resume damping down when fruit starts to swell — stop feed when the fruits start to show colour. Strawberries are ready for picking as soon as they are red all over — nip the stalk between thumbnail and forefinger. Varieties which are successful under glass include Elvira and Cambridge Favourite.

Strawberry

CHAPTER 3
CARE

WATERING

A greenhouse is a rainless place which relies on you for water. This task is more time-consuming than any other aspect of greenhouse growing, and it is probably the most difficult to master. The timing and amount to apply depend on so many things — a partial list includes plant type, season of the year, size of pot, temperature, compost type and air humidity.

There are no firm rules, but there are a number of points for general guidance. Among the basic things to remember is that roots need air as well as water, which means that compost should be moist but not saturated. Many flowering pot plants are happy to be kept moist at all times — other plants (e.g foliage house plants) need a period of drying out between waterings.

Watering is generally needed when the top ½ in. of compost has dried out — growing bags have their own special rules and these are printed on the pack. Another tip is to water to the weather. In summer plants may need watering twice a day — in winter they may require water only once a fortnight. Dormant plants need hardly any water during the winter months. Remember that plants need much more water on a sunny day than on a cloudy one. For example, a 3 ft Tomato plant loses only ½ pint on a dull day, but this rises to 2½ pints on a sunny day. Water in the morning, especially in cool weather. Try to avoid watering when the sun is shining brightly.

Tap water is suitable for nearly all plants, but for delicate plants it should be left to stand overnight. Do not use hard water on lime haters such as Azalea, Orchids, Cyclamen and Hydrangea. Rainwater is excellent, but it must be clean and not stagnant.

Manual methods

WATERING CAN

Insert spout **under** the leaves — pour water steadily and gently. Fill the space to the top of the pot — leave to drain.

A watering can enables you to satisfy individual needs better than any other method, but it is only practical for a small collection. Buy a 1 gallon good-quality can — the spout should be long and an extension spout is a useful extra. Use the spout for watering established plants — a fine rose for seedlings.

HOSE PIPE

Use a fine and gentle spray for seedlings

A hose pipe with a variable spray attachment will save you a lot of time. Use a gentle trickle for individual pots — turn it full on and you will wash compost out of the pots.

Automatic methods

There are several ways of making watering easier — the **automatic** ones work from the mains and all the plants are kept watered until the system is switched off. Nearly all amateur set-ups are **semi-automatic** — the reservoirs have to be filled manually and may need switching on each time water is required. All are great time savers, but all plants receive the same amount of water — a problem in a mixed collection in summer and a definite menace in winter.

CAPILLARY BENCH

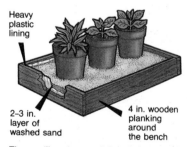

Heavy plastic lining

2–3 in. layer of washed sand

4 in. wooden planking around the bench

The capillary (or sand) bench has been around for many years, but it has never become popular. The staging holding the tray must be level and stout. The sand is kept moist by means of a watering can or a pipe connected to a manually-filled reservoir or mains-fed header tank. Plastic (not clay) pots without crocks are screwed into the moist sand.

CAPILLARY MATTING

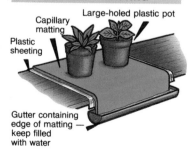

Large-holed plastic pot

Capillary matting

Plastic sheeting

Gutter containing edge of matting — keep filled with water

A modern alternative to the capillary bench — lighter, easier to install and more popular, but it has to be replaced after a time as it becomes clogged with algae. Polythene sheeting is laid on the bench and the matting is placed on top of it — this is kept permanently moist by means of a watering can, pipe fed by header-tank, or a water-filled gutter.

TRICKLE IRRIGATION

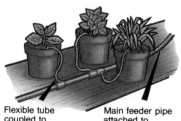

Flexible tube coupled to feeder pipe

Main feeder pipe attached to mains-fed tank

Greatly favoured by commercial growers, but an unsightly technique for a display greenhouse. The main pipe is fed from a header tank and small pipes wind from this in spaghetti-like fashion to exit points inserted in each pot. Water trickles into each pot either continuously or on a time-controlled basis. Check frequently for blockages.

VENTILATING

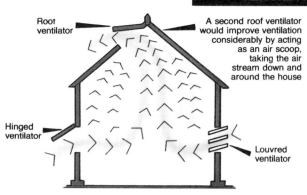

Root ventilator

A second roof ventilator would improve ventilation considerably by acting as an air scoop, taking the air stream down and around the house

Hinged ventilator

Louvred ventilator

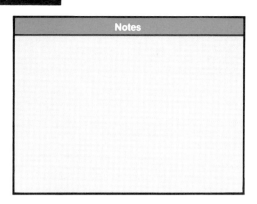

Notes

The need for at least one roof ventilator and one side ventilator in even a small house was stressed on page 5. Without them you will lose the battle against plant-harming high temperatures in midsummer, but this is not the only time when ventilation is required.

In a well-stocked house ventilation will be required almost all year round. In winter the roof ventilator should be opened an inch or two for a few hours around midday if the weather is dry and above the minimum temperature of the house — do this on the side away from the wind. The purpose is to reduce air humidity and keep the atmosphere buoyant — cold, humid and stagnant air in winter is the basic cause of grey mould and other diseases. This winter ventilation is vital if you are using a paraffin, gas or oil heater.

As spring arrives the roof ventilator is opened more widely and for longer in the day but the side ventilators are still kept closed — moving cold air rapidly over foliage will damage growth. In May the situation changes — the main purpose of ventilation is to keep the temperature below 75°F. Side ventilators are now opened, and it may be necessary to open the door as well.

In high summer ventilation is not enough to keep temperatures below the plant-damaging 85°F mark. Shading is necessary and so is regular damping down. It may be necessary to leave the ventilators open all day and all night, but a change in weather can mean closing a ventilator or two at night and for part of the day. Thus daily control is often necessary, and this makes the automatic ventilator a boon for all greenhouse owners. An extractor fan is much less vital, but it can be a godsend in an abnormally hot summer.

DAMPING DOWN

The traditional method of damping down has been carried out since the early days of greenhouse growing. The ritual begins as temperatures rise in late April or May — a hose pipe is used to wet the floor and benches. Once a day at first, but as often as three times a day in midsummer. On hot days the plants may be syringed with water.

As the water evaporates the temperature of the house is lowered — a basic benefit of damping down. But there are other benefits — the increase in air humidity means that water loss through the leaves is reduced, resulting in a lower requirement for frequent watering, and moisture-loving plants are able to survive. Furthermore dry-air pests such as red spider mite and thrips are kept in check and fruit set of Tomatoes is encouraged.

The problem with the traditional method is that the benefits are temporary on a hot day with all the ventilators open. Professional growers use electrically-driven humidifiers to provide a continual source of water vapour — for the amateur a continually damp area can be created by laying down capillary matting (see page 28) on the staging.

Automatic methods

AUTOMATIC VENTILATOR

The automatic ventilator is an additional cost, but buy one or more if you can afford it — this non-electric piece of equipment is an essential item if you don't spend every day at home. The heart of the unit is a tube containing a heat-expanding compound — this operates a plunger which opens or closes the ventilator as the temperature changes.

EXTRACTOR FAN

An extractor fan is set close to the ridge at the end opposite to the door. This item is a horticultural version of the domestic extractor fan. It is a low-speed model which does not create strong draughts but still creates enough air movement to remove hot and cold pockets in the house. A thermostat switches on the fan when the air reaches a set temperature.

HEATING

The unheated or cold greenhouse is a place for Tomatoes and Cucumbers in summer, Chrysanthemums in autumn and Alpines, Bulbs and Cacti in winter. Some form of heat is needed if you wish to extend this range — the usual plan is to maintain a minimum temperature of 42°–45°F (cool greenhouse) during the depths of winter. The ordinary gardener can forget about higher temperatures — the fuel costs are prohibitive.

A wide choice of fuels is available — coke, coal, wood, natural gas, bottled gas, oil and electricity. Gone are the days when everyone had to rely on hot water pipes heated by a coal- or coke-fed boiler. Nowadays the popular choices are paraffin, bottled gas and electricity. The appeal of paraffin is obvious — heaters are inexpensive and you don't need an electric cable. Still, the problems outweigh the advantages — thermostatic control is not practical and regular attention is essential. Bottled gas heaters are more satisfactory, but the large cylinders are heavy and the heaters are large and cumbersome. Electricity is generally considered the best source of heat — clean, easily controlled and disease-promoting humidity is not produced. A word of caution — installing electricity outdoors is a job for a professional electrician.

Whatever form of fuel you use, economy is essential. There are several ways to reduce the bill. Efficient insulation (page 62) can halve the heat loss and cut fuel bills by a third. Make sure that all cracks and ill-fitting windows are repaired so as to eliminate draughts and don't raise the temperature higher than necessary. Consider partitioning off some of the greenhouse if only part is in use.

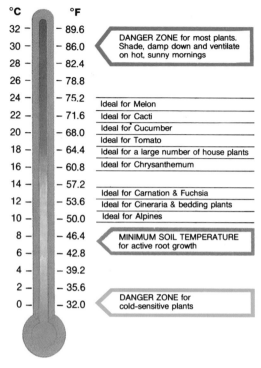

°C	°F	
32	89.6	DANGER ZONE for most plants. Shade, damp down and ventilate on hot, sunny mornings
30	86.0	
28	82.4	
26	78.8	
24	75.2	
22	71.6	Ideal for Melon
20	68.0	Ideal for Cacti / Ideal for Cucumber
18	64.4	Ideal for Tomato / Ideal for a large number of house plants
16	60.8	Ideal for Chrysanthemum
14	57.2	
12	53.6	Ideal for Carnation & Fuchsia / Ideal for Cineraria & bedding plants
10	50.0	Ideal for Alpines
8	46.4	MINIMUM SOIL TEMPERATURE for active root growth
6	42.8	
4	39.2	
2	35.6	
0	32.0	DANGER ZONE for cold-sensitive plants

Types of Greenhouse

COLD GREENHOUSE
Unheated except by the sun

minimum temperature 28°F when outside temperature falls to 20°F
Overall benefits: Plants are protected from wind, rain and snow
Growth is approximately 3–4 weeks ahead of outdoor plants
Drawbacks: No growth occurs in the depths of winter
Unsuitable for overwintering frost-sensitive plants

COOL GREENHOUSE
Heated during the cooler months

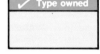

minimum temperature 42°–45°F
Overall benefits: Plants are protected from wind, rain, snow and frost
Growth is approximately 3–4 weeks ahead of cold greenhouse plants
Minimum temperature is just high enough to support plant growth
Frost-sensitive plants can be overwintered
Drawback: Fuel costs are £100–£150 per year for an average-sized greenhouse

WARM GREENHOUSE
Heated at night during most months

minimum temperature 55°F
Overall benefits: A wide range of plants can be grown during the winter months
Exotic flowers, vegetables and fruits can be grown
Drawback: Fuel costs are about three times higher than cool greenhouse costs

STOVE HOUSE
Heated at night all year round

minimum temperature 65°F
Overall benefit: Tropical plants can be grown — definite one up on the Jones's
Drawbacks: Fuel costs are prohibitive for the average gardener
Too warm for some plants

✓ Type owned

THE COLD GREENHOUSE

Avoid as much heat loss as you can during the winter months. Keep the glass clean to ensure maximum entry of the sun's rays and try to conserve as much of this heat as possible. Seal cracks to prevent draughts and repair broken lights and ill-fitting doors. About 80 per cent of the heat is lost through the glass, so line the sides and roof with polythene sheeting — see page 62. Plants in cold and wet soil can quickly rot or become diseased — keep the compost or soil on the dry side in winter. Some ventilation will be required as stagnant air encourages fungal diseases.

In the late spring and summer the problem is reversed — the temperature has to be reduced to keep the plants cool. Dry heat is more dangerous than moist heat, and several interlinked methods are used to lower temperatures. Damping down (spraying the floors with water on warm summer mornings) and misting the plants will lower the temperature when the house is adequately ventilated. As soon as temperatures continually rise above 75°F it is essential to shade the glass.

THE COOL GREENHOUSE

Make sure the heater you choose is sufficiently large to heat the greenhouse to 45°F when the temperature outside is only 20°F.

There are several formulae to calculate the size of heater required to ensure this capacity. Use the simple one below, after having worked out the surface area as shown on page 5.

	Size of heater required
Surface area x 33	BTUs per hour
Surface area x 10	Watts

As an example, an 8 ft x 6 ft house (surface area 208 sq. ft) requires 6864 BTUs per hour (paraffin, oil or gas) or 2080 watts (electricity) when the temperature is 20°F outside.

Your heater requirement	
Surface area	**sq. ft**
Paraffin, oil or gas heater **or** **electric heater**	**BTUs per hour** **Watts**

Types of Heater

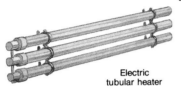

Electric
tubular heater

Electric fan heater
(horticultural type)

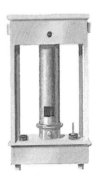

Paraffin
heater

Gas
heater

Electric
heating cable

Heat source	Details	✓ Type used
ELECTRIC FAN HEATER	The popular choice for a small greenhouse. There are many advantages — no fumes, no transport of fuel and good thermostatic control. These advantages are shared with other electric heaters, but fans have the added benefit of circulating the air quickly. Warm air is provided in winter, cool air in summer.	
ELECTRIC TUBULAR HEATER	The preferred type for heating a large house or where high temperatures are required. The warmth is distributed from the lines or banks of pipes around the walls although a single 'black heat' tube can be installed to warm up a cold spot. Heat is much more evenly spread than from a fan heater.	
ELECTRIC CONVECTOR HEATER	Convector heaters are very popular for home heating but have found little favour with greenhouse gardeners. This form of heater has neither the air-circulating properties of a fan nor the evenness of warmth of a tubular heater. Night-storage heaters are economical, but they provide day-heat when it is not necessary.	
PARAFFIN HEATER	Cheap to buy and generally cheap to run, but the advantages stop there. Water vapour is produced and this increases the risk of grey mould in winter. Buy a blue-flame model and trim the wick regularly. Make sure the heater is large enough to maintain a 42°F minimum. A useful standby in case of power failure.	
GAS HEATER	Flueless heaters are available which use either natural or bottled gas. They have their disciples — carbon dioxide is produced, which is beneficial to plants, and thermostatic controls are fitted. But there are drawbacks. As with paraffin the production of water vapour can be a problem and regular maintenance is essential.	
PIPED HOT WATER HEATER	The traditional type of greenhouse heater — once the standard and now very much the exception. Water is heated in a boiler by solid fuel, oil or gas and the hot water is circulated along horizontal pipes around the sides of the house. Pipes are 1½–4 in. in diameter. Heat distribution is excellent, but the system is costly to install.	
LINKED CENTRAL HEATING	Linking the greenhouse to the domestic heating system seems like an excellent idea if the greenhouse is a lean-to or conservatory. However home central heating systems operate during the day and switch off at night — the wrong way round for the greenhouse. Consult a central heating engineer if you decide to go ahead with this system.	
ELECTRIC HEATING CABLE	Two types are available. The more popular one is the soil-heating cable which is placed on the staging or in the soil. Economical, as the heat is directed exactly where you want it — frosting of plants in a bed in a cold house can be prevented. Also available is the air-warming cable, clipped on to the walls of a cold frame or small greenhouse.	

PLANTING

Once there were just two basic ways of growing plants under glass. Some flowers and small shrubs were kept in pots but most flowering perennials and shrubs (Chrysanthemum, Camellia etc) and the vegetables and fruits (Tomato, Cucumber, Grape, Fig etc) were grown in the border soil. The basic rules were followed — the ground was soaked with water a couple of days before and stakes were inserted before and not after planting.

The problem is that soils can become 'crop sick' when the same type of plant is grown year after year. Yields diminish and disease attacks increase alarmingly. When this happens you have to choose from several courses of action. You can change the soil, of course, or you can sterilise it with a garden disinfectant. Unfortunately, both are time-consuming, inconvenient and not always successful. Alternatively you can grow more plants in pots, but the popular answer is to change over to the modern technique of growing bag cultivation.

Growing bags have revolutionised greenhouse practice. They are consistent and sterile, and are capable of giving high yields. These compost-filled plastic bolsters are excellent for vigorous plants such as Tomatoes, Cucumbers and Melons, but you must follow the instructions carefully. The rules for watering and feeding are quite different from the way one cares for plants in border soil.

CLAY POT
Advantages: Less likely to topple over. Porous — less likely to waterlog. Traditional natural appearance

PLASTIC POT
Advantages: Less likely to break if dropped. Watering is needed less often. Decorative forms available

PEAT PELLET
Useful for seed sowing and potting on. Planted directly into soil or compost — no root disturbance. Compressed — soak in water before use

POLYTHENE SLEEVE POT
Inexpensive and easily stored. Useful as a stage in the potting on process. Usually thrown away after use but can be reused

PEAT POT
Useful for potting on before transfer to garden. The pot is bio-degradable. Planted directly into soil or compost — no root disturbance

POTTING

POTTING UP   This is carried out when a seedling or rooted cutting is ready to be transferred into its first pot — usually a 2½ or 3 in. clay or plastic pot. When dealing with seedlings ('pricking out') hold the delicate plant by a leaf and not by the stem.

POTTING ON   This is carried out when the roots have filled the pot and the plant is starting to become pot-bound. Matted white roots cover the rootball, and both stem and leaf growth have slowed down. Potting on into a larger pot is now necessary to encourage the plant to develop further.

① A suitable sequence of pot sizes is 3 in. → 5 in. → 7 in. → 10 in. Never miss out a stage in this sequence, but stop when the desired plant size is reached. Scrub out old pots — soak clay ones overnight.

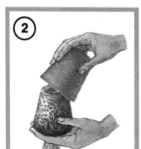

② Water the plant. One hour later remove it from the pot as shown above. If difficult to dislodge, knock pot on the edge of a table and run a knife around the rootball. Remove old crocks. Tease out matted roots.

③ Cover drainage hole of a clay pot with crocks. Add a layer of potting compost. Place the plant on top of layer — gradually fill surrounding space with damp potting compost. Firm compost with your thumbs.

④ Tap pot several times on table — leave ¾–1 in. watering space. Water carefully. Keep in the shade for a week — mist the leaves daily. Then place the plant in its growing quarters and treat normally.

RE-POTTING   This is carried out when the plant and/or pot has reached the desired or maximum size. Remove the plant as above and tease some of the old compost away from the rootball. Trim away some of the root tips, but do not reduce the rootball size by more than 20%. Pot up as described above, using the same size of pot. Wash the old pot thoroughly if it is to be reused.

TOP-DRESSING   This is carried out when you do not wish to or are unable to re-pot. In this case top-dress every spring by carefully removing the top 1–2 in. of compost. Replace the removed material with fresh potting compost.

FEEDING

Plants require food to remain healthy. A number of elements are involved, the main ones being nitrogen, phosphates and potash. This does not mean that plants need constant feeding — too much can be as harmful as too little. Commercial peat-based composts contain all the essential nutrients and these should last for about 6–8 weeks after planting. Feeding should then start, but how much and how often will depend on a number of factors.

Slow-growing and dormant plants need little or no food — actively-growing ones need feeding regularly. Liquid fertilizers are the best form for pot and growing bag plants — solid feeds should be confined to the border. Little and often is the golden rule — follow the manufacturer's instructions. As a general feed use a fertilizer in which nitrogen, phosphates and potash are in approximately equal proportions. Experienced gardeners, however, use more than one feed. A nitrogen-rich fertilizer such as Leaf Maker is used on foliage plants and on fruiting crops when leaf and stem growth are required. The plant needs change when the flowering and fruiting stages are reached. A high-potash feed is now called for — Flower Maker or Tomato Food is used to divert energy away from leaf production and into flower and fruit production.

Make sure that the compost is moist when feeding plants — applying fertilizer to dry compost can lead to injury. Foliar feeding is an interesting technique — dilute fertilizer is applied directly to the leaves. Make sure you use a product recommended for this purpose.

Feeding Guide

Use a compound fertilizer containing nitrogen, phosphates and potash. If there is no statement for one of them on the label then you can be sure it is missing.	
NITROGEN (N)	**The leaf maker** which promotes stem growth and foliage production. Needs to be balanced with some potash for flowering plants
PHOSPHATES (P_2O_5)	**The root maker** which stimulates active rooting in the compost. Necessary for both foliage and flowering types
POTASH (K_2O)	**The flower maker** which hardens growth so that flowering and fruiting are encouraged at the expense of leaf growth
TRACE ELEMENTS	Present in some house plant foods — derived from humus extracts or added chemicals. Shortage can result in discoloured leaves

Feeding Problems

Cause ▷	Too little fertilizer	Too much fertilizer
Effects ▷	Slow growth — little resistance to pests and diseases	Lanky and weak growth in winter — abnormal growth in summer
	Leaves pale with 'washed-out' appearance. Lower leaves drop — weak stems	Leaves wilted with scorched edges and brown spots
	Flowers absent or small and poorly coloured	Excessive leaf production may mask floral display

LIGHTING

It is lack of light as well as low temperatures which cause plant growth to slow down or stop in winter. This is not just a matter of dull days — day length is also important. Most plants need illumination for 12–16 hours in order to maintain active growth, which is why the resting period of foliage plants is not broken by a series of bright days in winter.

Installing fluorescent lighting has several advantages in winter. The increase in the duration and intensity of light boosts seedling and young plant growth and also induces flowering in some types — African Violets can be kept in bloom almost all year round. The most important advantage, however, is that you can work in the greenhouse during the long winter evenings. Use Gro-Lux tubes and fix a reflector above them. The tubes should be about 12 in. above the tops of the plants.

SHADING

In summer your greenhouse can become a death trap for plants. Many types are damaged when temperatures stay over 90°F, and others such as Begonia, African Violet and Gloxinia are scorched by summer sunshine.

The obvious answer is to install roller blinds of wooden slats, hessian or plastic. Outside slatted blinds are the best, but they are also the most expensive. The automatic version operated by a photo-electric cell is the height of glasshouse luxury, unlike the automatic ventilator which is a near-essential. Internal blinds are cheaper, but they are less efficient and cannot be used where plants are grown against the glass.

Another way to protect your plants from sun scorch is to paint or spray the outside with Coolglass. This is not removed by rain but can be easily wiped off with a duster during dull spells or at the end of summer.

PROPAGATING

You can, of course, buy seedlings and rooted cuttings for growing in your greenhouse. Even the most experienced and energetic gardener will do so occasionally, but you will miss much of the thrill of growing under glass if you don't learn the craft of propagation.

Propagation enables you to raise new plants from seeds and cuttings. You will save money, but there is more to it than that. The choice of seed varieties is infinitely greater than the range of seedlings on offer. Taking cuttings from your own stock allows you to know what the new plants will look like, and you will also know that they have been raised from healthy plant material.

Seeds of some important greenhouse crops, including Cucumber and Tomato, require a temperature of 60°–70°F to germinate satisfactorily. Cuttings require a moist and reasonably warm atmosphere in order to root satisfactorily. Obviously it would be ridiculous to create these conditions throughout the greenhouse during the cooler months of the year — a heated propagator (see page 5) is the answer.

Sowing seeds and striking stem cuttings are the more popular but not the only ways of propagating plants for greenhouse cultivation. Begonia rex and African Violet are propagated from leaf cuttings, Strawberries are reproduced by pegging down runners, clumps of Ferns are divided and small bulblets (offsets) are planted after removal from the sides of mature Bulbs.

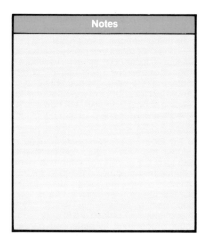

Notes

Sowing Seeds

1 **SEED** You must start with good quality seed. Buy from a reputable supplier and don't open the packet until you are ready to sow. Store unused seed in a screw-top jar — put it in a cool and dark place. Do not store opened packets of pelleted or dressed seed. Saving and sowing seed from your own plants often gives disappointing results — do not save seed from F_1 hybrids.

2 **CONTAINER** Use a seed tray, pan or ordinary flower pot. Drainage holes or cracks are necessary. Wash used containers thoroughly before filling — soak clay pots overnight.

3 **COMPOST** A peat-based seed compost provides an ideal medium for germination — sterile, light and consistent. Fill the container with seed compost or Multicompost. Firm lightly with a piece of board. Sprinkle the compost with water the day before seed sowing — it should be moist (not wet) when you sow the seeds. Scatter them thinly and cover with a thin layer of compost — small seeds should not be covered. Firm lightly with a board.

4 **COVER** Put brown paper over the tray or pot and place a sheet of glass over it. Condensation is absorbed by the paper and so does not drip on to the compost below. Change the paper if necessary.

5 **WARMTH** Some garden seeds will germinate quite happily at 50°F or less, but most greenhouse types require 60°–70°F for satisfactory germination. You cannot expect to maintain such temperatures in the glasshouse in spring, so you have two choices. A heated propagator is the more satisfactory answer, but if one is not available you can place the pot or tray on the windowsill of a centrally-heated room which is kept above the recommended minimum temperature.

6 **LIGHT** As soon as the seedlings break through the surface, remove the paper and prop up the sheet of glass. After a few days the glass should be removed and the container moved to a bright but sunless spot. Keep the compost moist but not wet.

7 **PRICK OUT** As soon as the first set of true leaves has opened the seedlings should be pricked out into trays, pans or small pots filled with potting compost. Handle the plants by the seed leaves — not the stems. The seedlings should be set about 1½ in. apart. Keep the container in the shade for a day or two after pricking out.

Correct stage for pricking out

8 **HARDEN OFF** When the seedlings have recovered from the pricking out move they can be moved to their allotted part of the greenhouse, but do shade in sunny weather until they are past the seedling stage. Seedlings destined to be transplanted outdoors must be hardened off to prepare them for life in the garden. Move the pots to the coolest part of the greenhouse and then to a cold frame. Keep the lights closed at first, then open during daylight hours. Finally, let the pots stand uncovered all the time for about 7 days before planting out.

Taking Cuttings

A cutting is a small piece removed from a plant which with proper treatment can be induced to form roots and then grow into a specimen which is identical to the parent plant. Some woody plants are difficult or impossible to propagate without special equipment, whereas cuttings of some popular house plants such as Ivy and Tradescantia will form roots in a glass of water. Early summer is the time recommended for many plants, but late summer is the popular time for Fuchsia and Pelargonium. So don't guess what to do — consult guides such as The House Plant Expert, The Flower Expert and The Tree & Shrub Expert.

There are a few general rules. Plant non-succulent cuttings as soon as possible after severing from the parent plant and make sure that the compost is in close contact with the inserted part. Keep the cuttings in an enclosed environment to maintain high air humidity around the plants — Cacti, Succulents and Pelargonium are exceptions. Finally, do not keep tugging at the cutting to see if it has rooted — the appearance of new growth is the best guide.

Softwood cuttings are green at the tip and base, and are taken from early spring to midsummer. Many hardy perennials and some small shrubs are propagated in this way. Basal cuttings are shoots formed at the base of the plant and pulled away for use as softwood cuttings in spring.

Semi-ripe cuttings are green at the top and partly woody at the base — they are usually heel cuttings (see below). Midsummer to early autumn is the usual time and most shrubs and perennial climbers are propagated by this method.

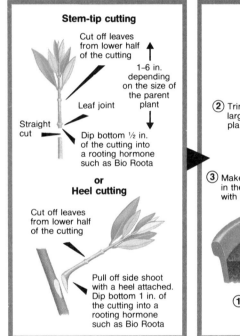

Stem-tip cutting

Cut off leaves from lower half of the cutting

1–6 in. depending on the size of the parent plant

Leaf joint

Straight cut

Dip bottom ½ in. of the cutting into a rooting hormone such as Bio Roota

or
Heel cutting

Cut off leaves from lower half of the cutting

Pull off side shoot with a heel attached. Dip bottom 1 in. of the cutting into a rooting hormone such as Bio Roota

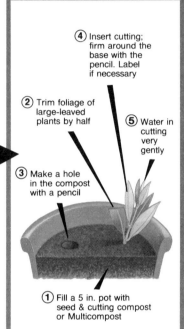

④ Insert cutting; firm around the base with the pencil. Label if necessary

② Trim foliage of large-leaved plants by half

⑤ Water in cutting very gently

③ Make a hole in the compost with a pencil

① Fill a 5 in. pot with seed & cutting compost or Multicompost

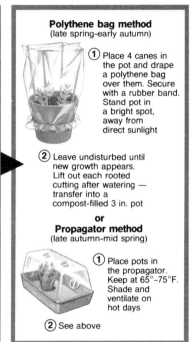

Polythene bag method
(late spring-early autumn)

① Place 4 canes in the pot and drape a polythene bag over them. Secure with a rubber band. Stand pot in a bright spot, away from direct sunlight

② Leave undisturbed until new growth appears. Lift out each rooted cutting after watering — transfer into a compost-filled 3 in. pot

or
Propagator method
(late autumn-mid spring)

① Place pots in the propagator. Keep at 65°–75°F. Shade and ventilate on hot days

② See above

Propagation Record

Date	Variety	Results

KEEPING PLANTS HEALTHY

The warm and moist conditions within a greenhouse provide a paradise for many pests and diseases. Few natural enemies are present and the breeding rate of plant-damaging organisms can be amazingly high. Of course there are times when you will have to spray or ignite a smoke, but a great deal can be done to prevent problems — if you follow the rules of good hygiene.

Prevent trouble before it starts

DON'T BRING TROUBLE INTO THE HOUSE

● Never use unsterilised soil. Buy a specially-prepared compost which you can be sure will be pest- and disease-free. Alternatively sterilise soil if you wish to prepare your own compost. Don't use unsterilised manures.

● Inspect new plants carefully and take any remedial action which may be necessary before putting them with other plants.

KEEP THE HOUSE CLEAN

● Do not leave rubbish laying about — remove dead leaves, old compost etc from benches and floor. Wash and neatly stack pots and trays after use.

● Cracks and woodwork can harbour pests and diseases, so clean down the house thoroughly once a year — see page 60. Use a garden disinfectant — follow the label instructions carefully.

FOLLOW GOOD GROWING PRACTICE

● Ensure that the house is properly ventilated. Dry air encourages pests such as red spider mite and thrips — saturated air encourages diseases.

● Water in the morning so that leaves can dry before nightfall. You can water in the early evening if the weather is warm.

● Do not use dirty rainwater — you can introduce pests, diseases and slime organisms in this way.

● Sterilise border soil annually to prevent the build-up of harmful organisms.

● Feed the plants regularly — potash is important.

INSPECT THE PLANTS REGULARLY

● Look for the first signs of trouble — pay special attention to the underside of leaves. Remove dead flowers and foliage promptly — take dead and dying plants out of the house.

● If there are problems take immediate action — see below.

Tackle trouble without delay

DO NON-SPRAYING JOBS FIRST

● Minor attacks by caterpillar and leaf miner can be controlled by hand picking. Mouldy leaves and fruits should be removed at once.

● Many problems are due to poor growing conditions rather than a specific pest or disease. Improve growing practice.

● Place a 2 in. layer of moist peat around the stems of Tomatoes and Cucumbers if damaged root action is suspected.

BUY THE RIGHT TREATMENT

● Spraying, fumigating or dusting may be necessary. Pesticides are safe to use in the way described on the label, but you must follow the instructions and precautions carefully.

● Make sure that the product is recommended for use under glass and for the plant in question. Cucumber, Melon, Begonia etc may appear in the 'do not spray' list.

TREAT IN THE RIGHT WAY

Do not spray or fumigate when the sun is shining. Close all ventilators before using a smoke

Take care with aerosols. Spraying too closely will cause scorch

Leaves should be dry

Use a fine forceful spray. It is wise to keep all sprays off your skin. Wash off any splashes

Do not spray open delicate blooms

Spray thoroughly both above and below the leaves until the leaves are covered with liquid which is just beginning to run off

FOLLOW THE AFTER-TREATMENT RULES

● Do not stay in the house after spraying. Lock the door after fumigating the house — open the ventilators and door the next day.

● Wash out equipment, and wash hands and face.

● Do not keep the spray solution to use next time.

● Store packs in a safe place. Do not keep unlabelled or illegible packs; throw in the dustbin after emptying liquid down an outside drain. Never store in a beer bottle or similar container.

INSECTS

ANTS
Ants steal seeds but do no direct injury to plants. However, they do carry aphids from plant to plant and also loosen soil around the roots. No action is usually needed, but you can use an Anti-Ant Dust along the runs.

APHID
Small, sap-sucking insects, usually green but may be black, grey or orange. A wide range of plants is attacked — the plant is weakened and viruses transmitted. Spray with Bio Sprayday — repeat as necessary.

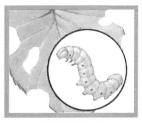

CATERPILLAR
Caterpillars of many types can attack vegetables and pot plants, but they are rarely a serious problem under glass. Pick off and destroy individual caterpillars — spraying with derris or fenitrothion is rarely necessary.

EARWIG
A familiar insect with brown body and pincer-like tail. Feeds at night on Carnation and Chrysanthemum leaves and petals. Trap in inverted straw-filled pots. Pick off when seen on the plants — shake flowers to remove.

EELWORM
Tomatoes and Chrysanthemums may be attacked by these microscopic, soil-living pests. Infested Tomato roots have corky swellings — Chrysanthemum leaves develop brown patches. Destroy the plants immediately.

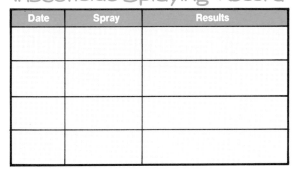

Insecticide Spraying Record

Date	Spray	Results

FUNGUS GNAT
The fungus gnat or sciarid is a tiny black fly which is harmless, but the eggs laid on the compost turn into minute maggots which attack young roots. Do not overwater — water the pot with malathion solution.

LEAF MINER
Long winding tunnels are eaten in the leaf tissue by small grubs. Chrysanthemum foliage is commonly attacked in this way. The carnation fly behaves differently, producing blotches on the leaves. Pick and destroy mined leaves.

MEALY BUG
Small pests covered with white, cottony fluff. Large clusters can occur on the stems and under the leaves of a wide variety of plants. Wipe off with cotton wool soaked in derris solution. For a severe infestation spray weekly with malathion.

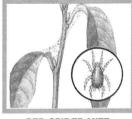

RED SPIDER MITE
Minute, sap-sucking pests which infest the underside of leaves of many greenhouse plants when conditions are hot and dry. The upper surface of the leaf becomes mottled — white webbing sometimes occurs. Mist daily. Spray with derris or Long-last.

SCALE
Small, brown discs are attached to the underside of leaves, especially along the veins. These immobile adults are protected from sprays by their outer waxy shells, but they can be wiped off with a damp cloth. After removal spray with malathion.

SLUGS
Irregular holes appear in the leaves of many plants and tell-tale slime tracks can be seen. These pests generally hide under rubbish, so keep the house clean. Scatter Slug Gard or Slug Mini-Pellets around damaged plants.

THRIPS
The tiny, black insects fly or jump from leaf to leaf, causing tell-tale silvery streaks on Begonia, Fuchsia etc. Damaged flowers are spotted and distorted. Spray with Bio Sprayday or derris at the first sign of attack.

VINE WEEVIL
The adult beetles attack leaves, but it is the 1 in. long grubs which do the real damage. They live in the compost and rapidly devour roots and bulbs. When plants wilt it is too late to apply control measures.

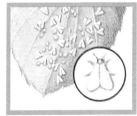

WHITEFLY
A serious and common pest — the larvae suck sap and deposit sticky honeydew. Badly infested leaves turn pale and drop. Hang up a yellow Greenhouse Fly Catcher or spray with Bio Sprayday — repeat as directed.

DISEASES

BLACKLEG
A disease of stem cuttings, especially Pelargonium. The base turns black, due to fungal invasion. The cause is overwatering or overcompaction of the compost. Remove infected cuttings — keep compost drier next time.

BLOSSOM END ROT
A leathery dark-coloured patch appears at the base of the Tomato — it frequently occurs where growing bags are used. The usual cause is drying out at a critical stage — keep the compost moist at all times.

BLOTCHY RIPENING
Parts of the ripe Tomato fruit remain yellow or orange — the cause is too much heat or too little potash. Prevent by applying Coolglass in hot and sunny weather, and by feeding regularly with a high-potash fertilizer.

BOTRYTIS (Grey Mould)
Grey fluffy mould which can cover all parts of the plant if the growing conditions are cool and humid. All soft-leaved plants can be affected. Cut away mouldy parts and spray with a systemic fungicide. Reduce watering and improve ventilation.

CROWN & STEM ROT
Part of the stem or crown is soft and rotten — known as basal rot when the base of the plant is affected. Nearly always fatal — throw the plant away. In future avoid overwatering and keep the plants in a warmer place.

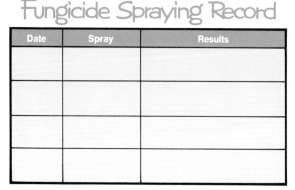

Fungicide Spraying Record

Date	Spray	Results

DAMPING OFF
The damping off fungi attack the root and stem base of seedlings. Shrinkage and rot occur at ground level and the plants topple over. Always use sterilised compost, sow thinly and never overwater. Remove affected seedlings.

GUMMOSIS
A serious disease of greenhouse Cucumbers — infected fruits develop sunken spots through which oozes an amber-like gum which goes mouldy. Destroy diseased fruit, raise temperature, reduce humidity and spray with Dithane.

LEAF SPOT
Brown moist spots appear on susceptible plants. In a bad attack the small spots enlarge and merge, killing the whole leaf. Burn infected leaves and keep the plants on the dry side for several weeks.

OEDEMA
Hard corky growths appear on the underside of leaves. This disease is not caused by fungi or bacteria — it is a response to waterlogged compost coupled with low light intensity. Reduce watering — improve illumination.

POWDERY MILDEW
A white powdery deposit spotting or coating the surface of the leaves. Unlike botrytis this disease is neither common nor fatal. Remove badly infected leaves and spray with a systemic fungicide. Alternatively dust with Sulphur.

ROOT ROT (Tuber Rot)
A fatal disease to which Cacti, Succulents, Begonias, Palms and African Violets are particularly prone. Yellowing and wilting of the leaves are followed by plant collapse. Next time be careful to avoid overwatering.

RUST
Not common — occasionally seen on Chrysanthemums, Fuchsias, Carnations and Pelargoniums. Powdery pustules occur on the underside of the leaves — burn infected leaves, increase ventilation and spray with Dithane.

SOOTY MOULD
A black fungus which grows on the sticky honeydew which is deposited by aphid, scale, whitefly and mealy bug. It is not particularly harmful — wipe off with a soft cloth and rinse with warm water. Spray to keep down insects.

VIRUS
There is no single symptom of virus infection. The growth may be severely stunted and stems are often distorted. Fruit may be misshapen and yellow blotches may appear on the leaves. There is no cure.

CHAPTER 4

DIARY

Many greenhouses are used to grow Tomato plants in summer, store a few house plants and produce seedlings in spring, and then little else for the rest of the year. Make your house earn its keep. Study this chapter and then plan for the year ahead — you can start at any time. Draw an outline of the greenhouse (1 box = 1 ft or 2 ft) and mark the plants you propose to grow.

WINTER

DECEMBER JANUARY FEBRUARY

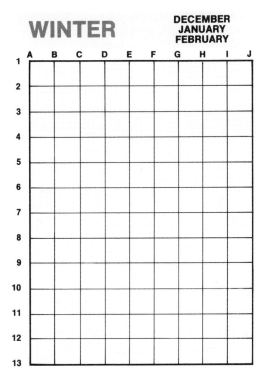

SPRING

MARCH APRIL MAY

SUMMER

JUNE JULY AUGUST

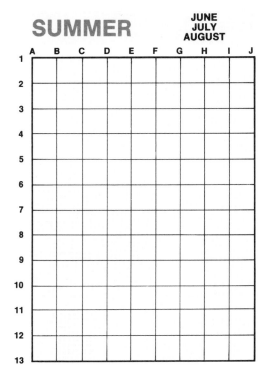

AUTUMN

SEPTEMBER OCTOBER NOVEMBER

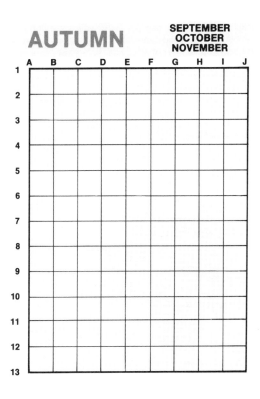

JANUARY

The start of a new year, but it's a slow start to the greenhouse year. The staging is usually at its emptiest — the Christmas pots went into the living room in December and the time for active seed sowing has not yet arrived. Only February is colder and only December has shorter days. Keep the greenhouse dry and reasonably cool and take the opportunity to get things ready for spring. This is a good time to take stock, checking on supplies and on the state of the structure. There are a number of jobs which can be done in January, but nearly all can be left until next month.

General Tasks

It is a good idea to draw up a plan for the coming year during this quiet period. Use the charts on page 39. Do grow more than just Tomatoes and bedding plants, but do not go to the other extreme of a jumble of plants with widely different requirements. Order seeds, composts etc. Check the greenhouse and its equipment. Block up all cracks which can lead to heat loss and draughts, and make sure that broken panes are quickly replaced. Inspect the heaters — paraffin stoves need regular filling and cleaning. Make sure that a max/min thermometer is installed at eye level.

Maintain a minimum temperature of 42°–45°F in the cool greenhouse if frost-sensitive plants are present. In a cold house it will be necessary to cover such specimens with matting if night frost is forecast. Do not aim for high temperatures — 55°–60°F during the day is high enough.

Maintain a dry atmosphere to prevent the onset of disease. Don't splash the floor, staging, leaves or the crowns of plants when watering. Pots should be watered sparingly — plants in flower should be watered more liberally. Water early in the day.

Inspect the plants. Keep pot plants which are in flower in a well-lit spot. Remove dead flowers and yellowing or diseased leaves. Spray if grey mould or whitefly has become a problem. Put down slug pellets if tell-tale shiny trails are seen.

Some ventilation is necessary, but do take care. The day should be dry and sunny — do not open ventilators on a damp or foggy day. Open ventilators on the side away from the wind — close the ventilators in mid-afternoon so as to conserve the heat of the sun before nightfall.

Complete insulation if not carried out last month — see General Tasks for December.

TEMPERATURE RECORD

Day	Minimum	Maximum

NOTES

On Display

Azalea indica

Arum Lily
Azalea
Begonia
Calceolaria
Camellia
Carnation
Cineraria
Cyclamen
Freesia

Hyacinth
Impatiens
Jasmine
Narcissus
Pelargonium
Poinsettia
Primula
Saintpaulia
Solanum capsicastrum

Camellia japonica

Bulbs

Bring in the bowls of spring-flowering bulbs (Hyacinth, Narcissus, Crocus etc) from the plunge bed outdoors. Choose the ones showing the most growth — leave the other bowls outdoors. Feed with weak liquid fertilizer when you water — take care not to overwater.

Plant Hippeastrum, Gloxinia and Achimenes.

Dust Gladiolus corms with Sulphur if disease spots are present.

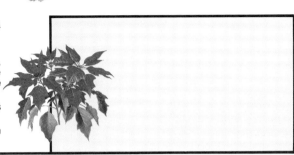

NOTES

Pot Plants

Sow seeds of Begonia, Pelargonium and Streptocarpus in a propagator.

Take Fuchsia and Chrysanthemum cuttings.

Pot on seedlings and rooted cuttings of Pelargonium, Fuchsia. Look at the Pelargonium cuttings — remove diseased leaves and throw away plants if the base of the stem has turned black.

Bring in pots of Polyanthus and container-grown Roses from the garden.

Prune Fuchsia and Passion Flower — cut back Charm Chrysanthemum after flowering.

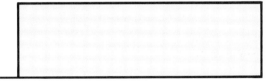

Bedding Plants

Inspect the pots of autumn-sown hardy annuals. Do not water unless the compost is distinctly dry on the surface.

Seed sowing of a number of bedding plants can begin in a heated propagator at the end of the month. Suitable types include Antirrhinum, Calceolaria, Canna, Carnation, Impatiens, Lobelia, Pelargonium and Verbena.

Garden Perennials & Shrubs

Look at the Dahlia tubers — dust with Sulphur if disease spots are seen.

Begin taking Chrysanthemum cuttings this month. Use new shoots growing from the base (not the sides) of the stems on the stool. The cuttings should be about 3 in. long.

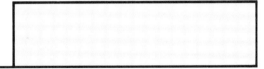

Tomatoes

The usual time for sowing Tomato seed is early March. However, in a heated greenhouse kept at a minimum night temperature of 50°–55°F, seed can be sown in a propagator in the first half of this month and then planted out in early March for a June crop.

Cucumbers   No work to be done this month.

Vegetables

Sow French Bean (*Masterpiece* or *Flair*), Lettuce (*Emerald*), Carrot (*Amsterdam Forcing*), Onion (*Ailsa Craig*) and Leek (*Lyon-Prizetaker*). Sow Cauliflower (*Snowball*) and Cabbage (*Hispi*) in a heated propagator.

Pot up and force Chicory — box up and force Rhubarb — see page 25.

Plant up early Potatoes in pots for a May crop.

Harvest Lettuce, Radish, Mushroom, Mustard & Cress, Chicory and Rhubarb.

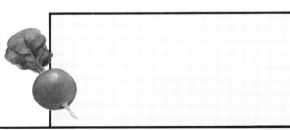

Fruit

Grape vines can be started into growth at the end of the month if a minimum night temperature of 45°F can be maintained.

Complete the planting of Peach, Nectarine and Apricot. Keep established plants cool and well-ventilated.

Bring pots of Strawberries into the greenhouse — keep in a well-lit spot.

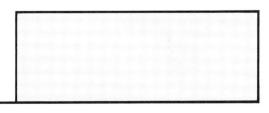

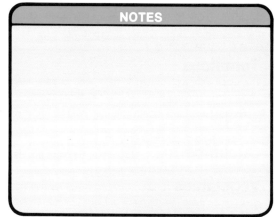

FEBRUARY

Both day length and jobs to be done increase this month, although the temperature outdoors is at its lowest ebb. Seed sowing begins in earnest — bedding plants which like a long time to establish are sown now and so are vegetables which are to be planted outdoors in cloche-warmed soil. There are Chrysanthemum and Dahlia cuttings to take, some potted shrubs to top-dress and others to start into growth. It is still too early to sow Tomato seed for the cold house and it is not yet time for sowing Cucumber. The season has started, but the busy months are still to come.

General Tasks

Lengthening days mean that the frequency of watering should be increased slightly compared with December and January, but you will still have to take care. Throughout the whole of the November–February period the soil should be kept on the dry side and water should be kept off the leaves and crowns. Watering from below is recommended whenever possible. This calls for placing the pots in a bowl of water and leaving them there until the surface of the compost glistens. Remove the pots and allow to drain before returning them to their growing quarters. When watering from above put the spout of the watering can under the leaves and try to do this task before midday.

●

Cover tender plants on cold nights if you can't maintain a minimum temperature of 42°F. Try to avoid wide fluctuations — aim to keep the air within a fairly narrow (42°-60°F) temperature range.

●

Keep the atmosphere dry. Ventilate on bright days, following the instructions listed under General Tasks for January.

●

Inspect the plants. Keep plants which are in flower in a well-lit spot. Remove dead flowers and yellowing leaves. Spray if pests or diseases appear.

●

Make sure that pots and seed trays are sterilised before use — wash with a garden disinfectant. Check that insulation is intact.

●

Label all seed trays clearly after sowing — don't trust your memory. Remember to sow thinly in damp (not wet) compost and to cover the container until germination has taken place.

TEMPERATURE RECORD		
Day	Minimum	Maximum

NOTES

On Display

Begonia	Impatiens
Calceolaria	Iris reticulata
Camellia	Jasmine
Carnation	Mimosa
Cineraria	Narcissus
Clivia	Pelargonium
Cyclamen	Primula
Freesia	Saintpaulia
Hyacinth	Tulip

Cineraria hybrid

Calceolaria herbeohybrida

Bulbs

Bring in the remainder of the bowls of spring-flowering bulbs from the plunge bed outdoors. Feed with weak liquid fertilizer when you water — take care not to overwater.

Plant Begonia, Hippeastrum, Gloxinia, Gloriosa and Achimenes in a cool greenhouse.

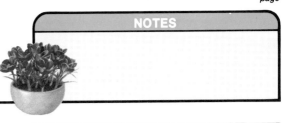

NOTES

Pot Plants

If you have a propagator a number of pot plants can be sown this month — Abutilon, Begonia, Celosia, Coleus, Streptocarpus, Saintpaulia, Pelargonium, Schizanthus and Solanum capsicastrum.

Take cuttings of Pelargonium, Carnation and Lorraine Begonias.

Pot on Ferns, Palms, Pelargonium, Fuchsia, Coleus and Schizanthus.

Prune Fuchsia, Bougainvillea and Pelargonium.

Bedding Plants

Pot on the autumn-sown hardy annuals.

A wide range of half-hardy annuals and other bedding plants can be sown this month rather than waiting until March. As a general rule small-seeded annuals are sown before the ones which have large seeds. Examples include Alyssum, Ageratum, Antirrhinum, Calceolaria, Celosia, Lobelia, Nicotiana, Pelargonium, Schizanthus, Sweet Pea, Stocks and Verbena.

Garden Perennials & Shrubs

Continue taking cuttings of Chrysanthemums. It is now time to start Dahlia tubers into growth in order to produce new shoots for cuttings. Box up the tubers in a damp peat/sand mix. Place in a well-lit spot and cut the shoots when they are 2–3 in. high. Propagate in the way described on page 17.

Bring the pots of dormant Hydrangea, Heliotrope and Fuchsia on to the staging. Bring them into growth by watering and exposing to maximum light.

Take cuttings of Heliotrope and Fuchsia.

Top-dress potted shrubs — remove the top inch of compost and replace with fresh material.

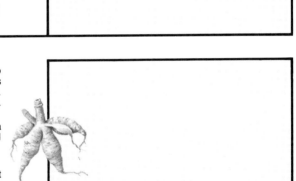

Tomatoes

Sow seed now if you failed to do so last month for planting in a cool greenhouse in late March or April.

Cucumbers   No work to be done this month.

Vegetables

Sow seeds for planting outdoors later in soil which has been covered with cloches. Included here are Broad Bean, early Pea, early Lettuce, Cauliflower, Carrot, Cabbage, Brussels Sprout, Onion, Parsnip and early Turnips.

Seeds can also be sown for growing to maturity in the greenhouse — examples are Lettuce and Aubergine.

Pot up and force Chicory.

Harvest Lettuce, Radish, Mushroom, Mustard & Cress, Chicory and Rhubarb.

Fruit

Sow Melon seed if heat can be provided.

Bring potted Strawberry runners into the greenhouse. Grow in 5 in. pots, growing bags or Strawberry pots.

Train Grape vines which started to grow last month. Hand pollinate flowers — see page 46.

MARCH

March is the start of the busy season. Most bedding and greenhouse pot plants can now be sown. Some seeds like Tomato, Melon and Cucumber need a heated propagator — others such as Antirrhinum, Lobelia and Petunia do not. Softwood cuttings can now be taken and the seedlings produced by last month's sowings need to be pricked out. Established plants begin to grow actively, so cultural practices change. Watering now takes place on a more regular basis and damping down of the floor and staging should start in the middle of the month.

General Tasks

Wide temperature fluctuations can be a problem this month — a bright sunny day at the end of the month can result in serious overheating. Aim to keep the air at 45°-65°F — this calls for heating at night and ventilating plus damping down on cloudless days.

●

Feed growing plants with a liquid fertilizer — do not overfeed young plants. Use a balanced rather than a high-potash formula for leaf growth — use a high-potash feed for flowering plants.

●

Seedlings need good light, but young ones will need shade from the midday sun.

●

Insects start to become a problem this month — keep watch for greenfly, whitefly and red spider mite. Spray with Sprayday or Derris before the problem gets out of hand.

●

Damping off is a soil-borne disease of seedlings — see page 38. It is much less of a problem these days with the introduction of sterile composts, but it still occasionally appears. This may be due to incomplete sterilisation of a soil-based compost, but it is much more likely to be caused by overwatering, use of dirty seed trays or sowing too thickly. Act swiftly — remove all toppled seedlings and water the rest with Cheshunt Compound solution.

●

Keep pots of growing plants damp but not soaking wet. Capillary matting is a great help — see page 28.

●

Flowers of Peach, Nectarine and Strawberries must be pollinated by hand as pollinating insects are absent. See page 46 for instructions.

●

Now is the time to prepare hanging baskets for setting out in late May or June.

TEMPERATURE RECORD

Day	Minimum	Maximum

NOTES

On Display

Begonia	Impatiens
Camellia	Jasmine
Carnation	Mimosa
Cineraria	Narcissus
Clivia	Pelargonium
Cyclamen	Primula
Freesia	Saintpaulia
Hippeastrum	Schizanthus
Hyacinth	Tulip

Primula obconica

Schizanthus hybrida

Bulbs

Once the flowers have faded, plant spring-flowering bulbs outdoors — do not keep for planting in bowls next year.

Start the following bulbous types into growth — Achimenes, tuberous Begonia, Caladium, Canna, Gloriosa, Gloxinia and Hippeastrum.

Sow Freesia seed.

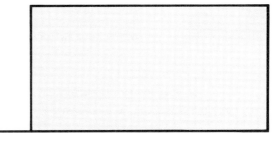

Pot Plants

Pot on autumn-sown plants into 5 in. pots — stake if necessary. Prick out seedlings raised from seed sown last month.

Sow seed of the types listed last month. Additional ones for March include Asparagus Fern, Cacti, Campanula isophylla, Capsicum annuum and Grevillea robusta.

Bring overwintered established plants into growth by increasing watering and bringing into full light.

Pot on Regal Pelargonium. Cut back Poinsettia when flowers have faded — keep dry until June.

Take cuttings of Coleus, Fuchsia and Pelargonium.

Bedding Plants

Prick out seedlings raised from seed sown last month.

Most bedding plants can be sown this month. Use last month's list — additional ones include Begonia semperflorens, Callistephus, Campanula, Iberis, Kochia, Ornamental Maize, Petunia and Salvia.

Start overwintered plants into growth — see Pot Plants above.

Garden Perennials & Shrubs

Continue to strike Chrysanthemum and Dahlia cuttings — pot on rooted cuttings which were taken earlier in the year. Pinch out the growing tips of rooted cuttings of Chrysanthemum when they are about 6 in. high — this will induce bushiness.

Plant Dahlia tubers not used for producing cuttings. Put them in a damp peat/sand mixture until buds have formed. Then cut up the root into planting pieces, each with at least one stout tuber and one stout shoot at the top. Plant in Multicompost.

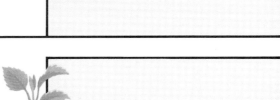

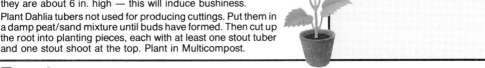

Tomatoes

Sow seed in a propagator for planting in a cold house in early May or for planting outdoors in late May or early June. The ideal germination temperature is 60°–65°F.

Prick out seedlings from a February sowing into 3 in. peat pots. Plant out seedlings from a December/January sowing when 6–8 in. high into growing bags or pots.

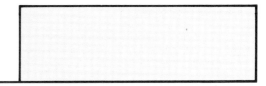

Cucumbers

Sow seed in a propagator for planting in a heated greenhouse in April.

Vegetables

A wide variety of seeds can be sown for planting out in the garden. See last month's list — extra ones include Courgette, Celery, Runner Bean, Sweet Corn, Leek and a number of herbs such as Parsley.

Seed can also be sown for growing to maturity in the greenhouse — examples include French Bean, Carrot, Lettuce, Capsicum, Aubergine and Beetroot.

Harvest Lettuce, Radish, Mushroom, Mustard & Cress and Chicory.

Fruit

Sow Melon and Cape Gooseberry.

Peach, Nectarine, Grape and perhaps Strawberry are in flower this month — hand pollinate as described in the General Tasks for April.

APRIL

Spring-flowering pot plants and bulbs in bowls should now provide an abundance of colour. Days are getting warmer, which means ventilation and damping down are necessary when the weather is sunny. There is lots of work to do. Seedlings must be pricked out before they become too large and cuttings must be potted on when new growth appears. This is the usual time to re-pot established plants and both Tomatoes and Cucumbers now need regular attention. Bedding plants must be prepared for their move outdoors at the end of next month or in early June.

General Tasks

High day temperatures can be a problem this month. Regular ventilation is essential. Open up the roof ventilators — don't use the bottom ones until the outside air gets warmer. Try to keep the greenhouse within the 45°–70°F range.

●

Some shading will be necessary in cloudless, sunny weather. This may mean coating part of the south-facing glass with Coolglass or covering small seedlings, newly-potted plants and rooted cuttings with newspaper during the heat of the day.

●

Check plants regularly to see if watering is needed. You may have to water actively-growing plants several times a week.

●

Keep watch for pests. Greenfly, whitefly, vine weevil and red spider mite are all active now. So are slugs, which can quickly destroy a trayful of seedlings.

●

Regular feeding of growing plants is essential. Follow the instructions on the package or bottle carefully. Little and often is the general rule — overfeeding can cause distortion, leaf damage or root scorch.

●

The need for night heating is reduced this month, but do take care. Young growth is especially susceptible to low temperatures — always ensure that the heaters are working whenever a frost is forecast. However, severe and prolonged frosts are not likely in the South, which means that insulation can now be removed as maximum illumination is essential.

●

Hand pollinate fruit. This calls for transferring pollen with a soft brush or a ball of cotton wool — do this work at midday. Repeat the procedure for several days to ensure success.

TEMPERATURE RECORD

Day	Minimum	Maximum

NOTES

On Display

Saintpaulia ionantha

Early Annuals	Jasmine
Azalea	Pelargonium
Carnation	Primula
Cineraria	Saintpaulia
Clivia	Schizanthus
Coleus	Schlumbergera
Freesia	Stephanotis
Hippeastrum	Streptocarpus
Impatiens	Tulip

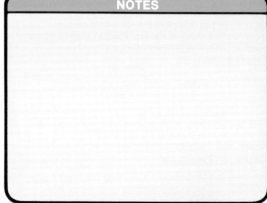

Stephanotis floribunda

Bulbs

Plant tuberous Begonia and Gloxinia.

Reduce watering when Cyclamen flowers fade. Remove and dry the corms — store for planting in autumn.

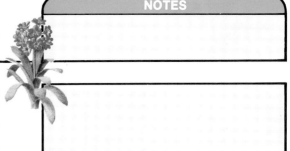

Pot Plants

Sow seeds of the types listed for February and March if this was not done at the recommended time. Prick out seedlings raised from seed sown last month.

Bring Hydrangea into growth by providing extra watering and warmth. Take stem cuttings.

Take cuttings of Pelargonium and Fuchsia if not done last month. Pinch out growing tips to induce bushiness.

April is the popular time for re-potting house plants and greenhouse pot plants. Follow the rules on page 32. With some types clumps can be divided when re-potting.

Bedding Plants

Sow seeds of the types listed for February and March if this was not done at the recommended time. Sow Zinnia, Nemesia and Marigolds. Sow Primrose and Polyanthus for garden display next spring.

Prick out seedlings raised from seed sown last month. Begin hardening off for planting outdoors at the end of next month.

Garden Perennials and Shrubs

Plant up Dahlia tubers if this was not done last month.

Pot on rooted cuttings. Take softwood cuttings.

Tomatoes

Plant out seedlings in a cold house — the Tomato plants should be about 6–8 in. high at this stage and the flowers of the first truss should be beginning to open. Seedlings which have not yet reached this stage should be potted on into 3 in. peat pots for planting out in May. Plants destined for planting outdoors in late May should be hardened off this month.

Tomatoes in growing bags need regular and frequent watering — follow the instructions carefully. Feed with Bio Tomato Food every time you water.

Pinch out side shoots. Mist plants at midday and tap the supports occasionally to aid pollination and fruit set.

Cucumbers

Plant out seedlings in a heated greenhouse before the end of the month. Sow seed to produce Cucumber seedlings for planting out in a cold house at the end of May.

Vegetables

Sow Marrow, Courgette, Runner Bean, Celeriac and French Bean for planting out in the garden at the end of next month or early June.

Plant Capsicum and Aubergine seedlings in growing bags.

Harvest Carrot, Lettuce, Radish, Mushroom, Mustard & Cress, Potato and Chicory.

Fruit

Plant March-sown Melon — sow seed now if this job was not done last month.

Start Grape vine into growth in a cold greenhouse — do this by increasing water and closing down ventilators.

Hand pollinate flowers as they appear. Thinning of young fruit of Grape, Peach, Nectarine and Strawberry may be necessary — do this in stages. Water liberally and regularly once fruit has started to swell.

Harvest Strawberry.

MAY

Shortage of space is often a problem this month. There are trays and pots of bedding plants, vegetables, shrubs and pot plants everywhere, and on the floor there are growing bags filled with Tomatoes and Cucumbers. The answer is to transfer bedding plants and vegetables into a cold frame to harden off for their move into the open garden at the end of the month. Daytime heating generally stops this month, but night frosts do occur, so don't put the heater away. Remember to space out pots so that fresh air will circulate round them.

General Tasks

Between November and April the major temperature problem was to keep the atmosphere above freezing point on cold nights. Now the main task is to keep the temperature of the air below 75°–80°F during warm and sunny spells.

●

Shading becomes important. Use blinds if you have them — otherwise paint the glass with Coolglass. Only the south-facing panes need to be treated at this stage — rub off if weather turns dull and cool.

●

In most parts of the country a heater will no longer be required during the day. But night frosts are still a possibility, so don't switch off at this stage.

●

Ventilation is vital this month. Open bottom or side ventilators as well as roof ones if the temperature is over 75°F — open the door if necessary.

●

Damp down the floors and staging in the morning when the weather is sunny. This water has two roles — the air temperature is lowered when it evaporates and the relative humidity is raised. See page 29 for more details.

●

Plants are now actively growing but roots in pots or growing bags cannot extend to seek out extra food as in the open garden. Regular feeding is therefore required — little and often is the golden rule. For general purposes use a balanced formula with nitrogen, phosphates and potash in roughly equal proportions. To stimulate leaf growth use a high-nitrogen feed — for plants in flower or fruit use a high-potash fertilizer.

●

Regular and thorough watering is essential — some plants will need daily attention. You must check the dryness of the compost every day if automatic watering is not installed.

TEMPERATURE RECORD

Day	Minimum	Maximum

NOTES

Achimenes hybrida

On Display

Achimenes	Impatiens
Annuals	Lily
Begonia	Pelargonium
Bougainvillea	Primula
Calceolaria	Saintpaulia
Carnation	Schizanthus
Celosia	Spathiphyllum
Cineraria	Stephanotis
Fuchsia	Streptocarpus

Impatiens wallerana

Bulbs

Plant Begonia, Canna and Gloxinia.

Reduce watering of Arum Lily, Freesia, Lachenalia and Nerine once the flowers have faded.

Pot Plants

It is now time to sow the seeds of plants for winter display in the home. Included here are Asparagus Fern, Calceolaria, Cineraria, Primula and Schizanthus.

Prick out seedlings raised from seed last month.

Take cuttings of house plants. Cuttings of Azalea, Coleus and many succulents are taken this month, but July and August are the usual months for striking Pelargonium cuttings.

Pot on rooted cuttings.

Bedding Plants

The main activity this month is hardening off. This calls for moving the seedlings into a cooler and fresher environment to get them used to the conditions they will have to face outdoors. This is done in several stages — the ideal steps are to place the trays in the coolest part of the greenhouse, then into a cold frame and finally to a sheltered part of the garden for a few days before planting out.

Sow Viola and Pansy for bedding out in autumn.

Garden Perennials & Shrubs

Rooted Chrysanthemum and Dahlia cuttings are planted out at the end of this month or in June. Harden them off during May to prepare the plants for outdoor conditions.

Tomatoes

In the cold greenhouse finish planting into growing bags seedlings which have started to flower.

Established plants are now growing actively. Feed regularly once the first fruits have started to swell and make sure that the compost is never allowed to dry out.

Train the stems up the vertical string. Remember to turn the twine around the stem, not the other way around.

Tap the supports or flowers daily to aid pollination. Pinch out the side shoots which appear where the leaves join the stem.

Cucumbers

Plant seedlings into growing bags in a cold greenhouse at the end of this month. Water carefully at first, keeping the compost damp but not wet. Increase watering when the plants start to grow actively — 2 pints a day per growing bag may be needed when the plants are in full growth.

Train the stems up vertical supports and pinch out unwanted growth — see Cucumber notes for June.

Vegetables

This is a time for cropping rather than sowing. Harvest Beetroot, Carrot, French Bean, Lettuce, Mushroom, Mustard & Cress and Potato.

Fruit

Plant Melon sown last month. Established plants need warm and humid conditions — damp down regularly.

Hand pollinate Melon and Grape vine when flowers appear. Thinning of Peach, Nectarine and Grape may be necessary — do this in stages using The Fruit Expert as your guide.

Pruning and training of Peach, Nectarine, Grape and Melon must be carried out this month. Don't guess what to do — follow carefully the rules set out in The Fruit Expert.

Harvest Strawberry.

JUNE

There is a marked change this month. Most of the pots and trays disappear in June as the vegetable seedlings, bedding plants, summer-hardy pot plants, tender shrubs, rooted perennials and hanging baskets are moved to their outdoor quarters. Tomatoes and Cucumbers now come into their own and there is much work to do — picking of the first fruits starts in the heated greenhouse. Heaters are switched off this month except in the colder part of the country — clean and overhaul heating equipment now instead of waiting until the onset of winter.

General Tasks

Sun scorch can be a problem this month — growth slows down, flowers lose their colour and leaves are scorched. Shading is the answer — use Coolglass.

●

Regular ventilation now becomes essential — open all ventilators and the door as required to keep the temperature down. Ventilation during the morning and evening should be carried out on warm days and it may be necessary to open a ventilator on warm nights. Automatic ventilation is a great aid, especially if you take long holidays and there is nobody to look after the greenhouse when you are away. Install it this month if you intend to buy one — do not wait any longer.

●

Check watering requirements daily. Some plants may need water twice a day. Feed at regular intervals.

●

You must damp down the greenhouse regularly by spraying the floor and staging in the morning or early afternoon. Apart from moistening the air and cooling the greenhouse there is the added benefit of discouraging red spider mite which can be a menace at this time of the year.

●

Plants destined for the garden are moved out this month — make sure that the danger of frost has gone before putting out half-hardy plants and also make sure that greenhouse-grown specimens have had a period of hardening off before the move into the garden. Some greenhouse plants can be stood out in the open garden during the June–early October period — this improves their health and gives you more space under glass.

●

Clean up after the big move outdoors. Do not leave dirty pots, discarded plants or dead leaves laying about.

TEMPERATURE RECORD

Day	Minimum	Maximum

NOTES

Streptocarpus hybridus

On Display

Achimenes
Annuals
Begonia
Bougainvillea
Callistemon
Carnation
Celosia
Clivia
Fuchsia

Gloxinia
Hippeastrum
Hydrangea
Impatiens
Lily
Pelargonium
Saintpaulia
Stephanotis
Streptocarpus

Hydrangea macrophylla

Bulbs

Sow Cyclamen — pot on seedlings raised earlier.

Reduce watering of Arum Lily when flowering has finished — dry and store bulbs.

Pot Plants

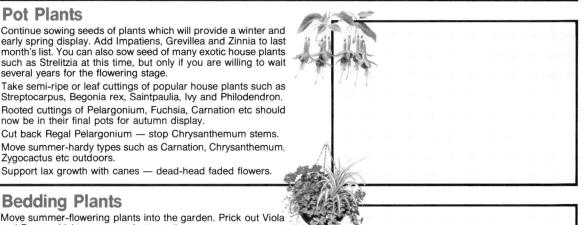

Continue sowing seeds of plants which will provide a winter and early spring display. Add Impatiens, Grevillea and Zinnia to last month's list. You can also sow seed of many exotic house plants such as Strelitzia at this time, but only if you are willing to wait several years for the flowering stage.

Take semi-ripe or leaf cuttings of popular house plants such as Streptocarpus, Begonia rex, Saintpaulia, Ivy and Philodendron.

Rooted cuttings of Pelargonium, Fuchsia, Carnation etc should now be in their final pots for autumn display.

Cut back Regal Pelargonium — stop Chrysanthemum stems.

Move summer-hardy types such as Carnation, Chrysanthemum, Zygocactus etc outdoors.

Support lax growth with canes — dead-head faded flowers.

Bedding Plants

Move summer-flowering plants into the garden. Prick out Viola and Pansy which were sown last month.

Garden Perennials & Shrubs

This is a good time to take cuttings of a number of garden perennials such as Gypsophila, Delphinium, Pinks and Lupin.

Sow hardy perennials now if you intend to raise them from seed.

Move out tender shrubs such as Citrus which have overwintered in the greenhouse. Also move out summer-hardy greenhouse shrubs such as Camellia and Hydrangea once flowering has finished.

Tomatoes

Continue to follow the rules laid down for May. Regular watering and feeding become even more important and so does the regular watch for pests and diseases.

Train the stems up the vertical supports — do this job in the morning. At midday tap the supports or mist the flowers gently to aid pollination. Continue to remove side shoots and cut off yellow leaves which are immediately below a fruit truss.

In a heated greenhouse the first fruits will be due for picking. See page 20 for instructions on how to tell when the fruit is ready for harvesting.

Cucumbers

In the cold house finish planting seedlings into growing bags.

Continue to follow the rules laid down for May. Regular watering and feeding are essential. Daily damping down is necessary. The tip of each side shoot should be pinched out at 2 leaves beyond a female flower. Pinch out tips of flowerless side shoots when 2 ft long. Remove all male flowers.

Picking starts this month in a heated greenhouse.

Vegetables

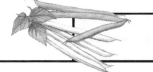

Sow French Bean and Mustard & Cress.

Harvest Beetroot, Carrot, French Bean, Lettuce, Mustard & Cress, Parsley, Radish and Mushroom.

Fruit

Water, feed and train Peach, Nectarine, Grape and Melon. Hand pollinate Melon.

Thin Grape bunches — see The Fruit Expert for details.

Harvest Strawberry.

JULY

Often the hottest month of the year, and one of the busiest in the greenhouse. Watering is a tiresome job which has to be done every day — so is the constant opening and closing of the ventilators. Still, this must be done if you do not have automatic systems installed — Tomatoes and Cucumbers can seriously suffer if subjected to one or two days' dryness, and a fully closed-down greenhouse in the middle of a heat wave can lead to damage or death of many plants. Holidays are a problem — you will need a friend or neighbour to take care of the plants in the greenhouse.

General Tasks

The major problem is keeping the temperature low enough during a hot spell. Opening all the ventilators and propping the door open may not be enough. Damping down and shading will help, but the answer may be to install an extractor fan or to bring in an electric fan to provide forced ventilation.

●

As in June sun scorch can be damaging. Some form of shading is essential for many plants — flowering pot plants, rooted cuttings, Cucumbers in flower etc. Inside blinds are difficult to use when tall-growing plants such as Tomatoes and Cucumbers are present. A shading paint such as Coolglass is an easier and less expensive answer.

●

Compost must be felt every day and watering carried out without fail. Daily damping down is needed.

●

Keep watch for pests and diseases. Red spider mite, greenfly, whitefly, thrips, grey mould and mildews are the major headaches — spray promptly if you see them, but read the rules for safe spraying (page 36) before you begin. Birds and egg-laying butterflies entering through open ventilators and door can pose a problem.

●

Routine feeding is necessary as most plants are now growing vigorously. A liquid feed at fortnightly intervals is suitable as a basic treatment, but fruit-bearing plants such as Cucumbers and Tomatoes need feeding every 7–10 days.

●

July is a good time for taking cuttings — roots usually form quickly in the warm conditions.

TEMPERATURE RECORD

Day	Minimum	Maximum

NOTES

Celosia plumosa

On Display

Achimenes	Heliotrope
Begonia	Hibiscus
Cacti	Impatiens
Calceolaria	Ipomoea
Canna	Passion Flower
Carnation	Pelargonium
Celosia	Saintpaulia
Fuchsia	Schizanthus
Gloriosa	Streptocarpus

Heliotrope hybrida

Bulbs

Summer-flowering bulbs make a fine show at this time of the year — Lilies, Gloxinia, Achimenes, Begonia, Canna, Gloriosa etc. When flowering has finished remove the seed pods before they develop so that all the energy is diverted away from the pods and into building up the underground storage organs.

Plant up Cyclamen and Freesia.

Pot Plants

Sow Stocks and Mignonette for winter scent and colour. Sow Coleus, Cineraria, Calceolaria, Schizanthus and Primula for a bright display next spring.

Prick out and pot on seedlings of winter-flowering annuals sown in May and June.

Pot on Fuchsia and Pelargonium.

Take cuttings of Regal Pelargonium, Saintpaulia, Impatiens, Coleus, Fuchsia and foliage house plants.

Stake and train climbing plants as necessary. Disbud large-flowering Begonia and Carnation for maximum display.

Move Solanum capsicastrum outdoors to stimulate berry formation.

Shade pot plants in flower.

Move out summer-hardy shrubs which were not transferred to the garden last month. It is important to move pot-grown Roses outdoors — others which should be strengthened by a stay outdoors include Camellia and Azalea.

Bedding Plants   No work to be done this month.

Garden Perennials & Shrubs

Cuttings of many garden shrubs can be taken this month — use semi-ripe wood and dip the ends in Bio Roota before inserting in the compost. Examples include Cotoneaster, Forsythia, Hydrangea, Philadelphus, Pyracantha and Weigela.

Tomatoes

Continue feeding, watering, damping down and ventilating as noted last month.

The plants will now be in full fruit and picking will be necessary nearly every day. Remove side shoots as they appear, but only remove the lower leaves if the greenhouse is well shaded.

Remove the tip at 2 leaves above the top truss when the plant reaches the top of the greenhouse or when 7 trusses have set. Top-dress plants growing in pots with fresh compost.

Cucumbers

The plants are now in full fruit — see page 21 for instructions on how to tell when the fruit is ready for harvesting.

Pinch out the growing point when the main stem reaches the roof.

Continue watering, damping down and ventilating as noted for May and June. Feed regularly with a Tomato fertilizer.

Vegetables

Sow Parsley and Mustard & Cress. Chit Potatoes for planting next month for a Christmas crop.

Harvest Lettuce, Radish, Capsicum, Mustard & Cress and Parsley.

Fruit

Train, feed and water as for June.

Thin Grape bunches — vines prefer a dry atmosphere.

Support Melon fruits with netting. Peg down Strawberry runners to produce new plants for next season.

Harvest Melon, Peach and Nectarine.

AUGUST

A well-planned greenhouse is an attractive sight in August — staging filled with colourful pot plants and a background of climbers, fruit, Tomatoes and Cucumbers. The problem of keeping the temperature down still remains, but this warmth means that the pots can be stood outdoors without coming to any harm. Because of this, August is often recommended as a painting and repair month, the plants being returned once the work is over. Use a water-based and not a solvent-type wood preservative for treating a wooden greenhouse.

General Tasks

Watch for grey mould — if leaves, fruit and flowers are attacked you should destroy affected parts, spray with a systemic fungicide and improve ventilation. Make sure that the plants are not splashed in the evening and never leave old leaves and fruit laying about. Dead-head flowering plants regularly to extend the flowering season.

●

Ventilation remains a vital task. Open all the ventilators and the door on warm days — during the night open only the roof ventilator.

●

Continue with the chore of regular watering. Daily soakings will still be needed for vigorous plants in small containers.

●

Routine feeding of actively-growing plants remains a necessity. Use a potash-rich feed to prolong and improve fruiting and flowering — leave 10–14 days between feeds.

●

This is a good month for taking cuttings for plants in the garden. There are three groups — Alpines such as Armeria, shrubs such as Weigela and half-hardy types such as Pelargonium. Don't take many more cuttings than you will be able to handle, but always strike a few extra as failures do occur.

●

The annual round of planting bulbs begins this month — make sure you have an adequate supply of pots, bowls and bulb fibre.

TEMPERATURE RECORD

Day	Minimum	Maximum

NOTES

Begonia multiflora

On Display

Begonia	Lantana
Campanula	Lily
Canna	Passion Flower
Carnation	Pelargonium
Celosia	Plumbago
Fuchsia	Saintpaulia
Heliotrope	Streptocarpus
Impatiens	Thunbergia
Ipomoea	Vallota

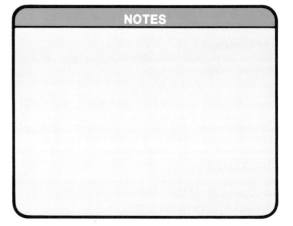

Campanula isophylla

Bulbs

Sow Cyclamen seed for flowering at Christmastime next year.

Plant up Freesia, Lachenalia, Nerium, Vallota, Cyclamen, Arum Lily and Iris reticulata.

At the end of the month plant up specially prepared bulbs of Hyacinth and Narcissus for blooming at Christmas.

After flowering dry off and store Hippeastrum, Achimenes, Gloxinia and Begonia.

Pot Plants

A key job this month is to sow a variety of hardy and half-hardy annuals to provide a spring display in the greenhouse. Choose from Schizanthus, Nemesia, Phlox, Clarkia, Primula, Salpiglossis, Cineraria, Larkspur and Sweet Scabious.

Prick out seedlings from July sowing — pot up rooted cuttings.

Take cuttings of greenhouse plants and climbers if these were not taken last month.

Pot up Cineraria and Primula for Christmas flowering.

Prune back climbing plants if the shade effect on other plants is becoming a problem.

Bedding Plants

Take cuttings from the tender bedding plants growing in the garden — Pelargonium, Fuchsia etc. The rooted cuttings are overwintered in the greenhouse for bedding out in late May-early June next year.

Garden Perennials & Shrubs

Continue to take cuttings this month of outdoor shrubs. Add Hebe, Escallonia, Laurus, Kerria, Hypericum, Euonymus, Erica, Cytisus and Lavender to last month's list.

Take cuttings of Alpines.

Tomatoes

Follow the cultural practices noted under May, June and July. Regular watering is vital — irregular watering reduces yield, produces cracked fruit and induces blossom end rot. Ventilation is needed to keep the temperature below 80°F.

Check that the wires and other supports are strong enough to support the weight of the plants and crop.

Never leave fruit on the ground — moulds will develop and the growing crop can be affected.

Continue with a regular feeding programme. Follow the manufacturer's instructions — with Bio Tomato Food you feed every time you water.

Cucumbers

Continue to water, damp down, ventilate and feed as described for May, June and July. You must feed regularly — use a Tomato fertilizer every 2 weeks.

Vegetables

Sow Winter Lettuce (*Kwiek* or *Marmer*), Carrot, Potato (see July notes), Endive and Chicory.

Harvest Lettuce, Capsicum, Aubergine, Radish, Mustard & Cress and Mushroom.

Fruit

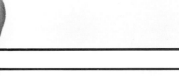

Water and feed Grape vine — use a Tomato fertilizer.

Reduce watering of Melon once the fruits have started to ripen.

Pot on rooted Strawberry runners — stand the pots outdoors.

Harvest Melon, Grape, Nectarine, Peach and Apricot.

SEPTEMBER

Days are shorter and nights are colder — the first days of autumn arrive this month. Many plants will still be actively growing, but the colourful summer display declines as the month progresses. Now is the time to start bringing in frost-sensitive plants from the garden and to prepare for the coming winter. Check the heating system — you may need to use it if there are early frosts. The Cucumber season finishes in September and most Tomato plants are removed — September is a good month for cleaning and disinfecting the greenhouse.

General Tasks

Temperature has to be carefully controlled this month. In an Indian summer you will have to open up all the ventilators and perhaps the door to avoid overheating, but during a cold snap all the ventilators should be closed. Aim to keep the temperature in the 50°-70°F range — close down the ventilators in early evening to retain some of the sun's warmth overnight.

●

Damping down as well as ventilation is reduced this month. Only spray the floor and staging on warm days, and even then make sure that the job is completed by midday.

●

Compost stays moist longer as temperatures fall — growth becomes less active. Reduce the frequency of watering accordingly.

●

Remove shading in late September — maximum illumination is now more important than heat control, but maintain some form of shading in areas where shade-lovers such as Ferns are present.

●

There may be a gap between clearing out the Tomatoes and Cucumbers and bringing in the frost-sensitive plants from outside. This may be at the end of this month or the beginning of October, and it is an excellent opportunity to fumigate the structure with a fungicidal smoke.

●

Don't wait too long before bringing in tender specimens — one sharp frost may kill them. Make sure that the pots of Chrysanthemum, Fuchsia etc are free from pests before the move indoors.

TEMPERATURE RECORD

Day	Minimum	Maximum

NOTES

Bougainvillea glabra

On Display

Abutilon	Impatiens
Begonia	Ipomoea
Bougainvillea	Passion Flower
Carnation	Pelargonium
Cobaea	Petunia
Exacum	Saintpaulia
Fuchsia	Stephanotis
Gloriosa	Streptocarpus
Gloxinia	Thunbergia

Pelargonium hortorum

Bulbs

Finish potting up prepared Hyacinth and Narcissus bulbs for Christmas flowering. Keep the bowls in a dark, frost-free shed or plunge them under a layer of peat or ashes outdoors.

Plant up Freesia, Lily, Cyclamen, Lachenalia, Hippeastrum and Arum Lily.

Finish sowing Cyclamen seed for flowering at Christmastime next year.

NOTES

Pot Plants

Pot up the annuals sown last month for spring display — it is still not too late to sow seeds if you failed to do so in August.

Bring in pot plants which have stood outdoors over the summer months. There is no great hurry if the weather is mild, but you should complete the task before the first frosts arrive. Plants involved include Chrysanthemum, Carnation, Azalea, Primula, Cineraria, Camellia, Zygocactus and Solanum capsicastrum.

Disbud Chrysanthemum.

Prune back climbers which have finished flowering.

Bedding Plants

Take cuttings of frost-sensitive bedding plants growing in the garden to provide material for planting out next year.

Plants such as Pelargonium, Heliotrope, Canna and Fuchsia which have not been used for cuttings should be dug and potted up. These plants are kept cool and on the dry side over the winter months, prior to bedding out again next year.

Sow hardy annuals such as Sweet Pea and Pansy for spring bedding in the garden.

Garden Perennials & Shrubs

Begin to bring in the tubs of tender shrubs and trees (e.g Orange and Lemon) which have stood outdoors throughout the summer months. Timing depends on beating the arrival of the first frosts.

September is a good month for taking cuttings of evergreens. Some types are difficult to propagate.

Tomatoes

Despite the cooler days it is as vital as ever to make sure that the compost never dries out. Ventilate to keep the temperature below 80°F on warm days and damp down as necessary.

Continue to pick fruit regularly. Remove leaves which are covering ripening fruits and never leave discarded Tomatoes laying about.

Cropping can continue until October but picking often stops at the end of this month. Place any remaining fruit on the windowsill to ripen. Remove old plants, growing bags, pots etc promptly — dead leaves encourage diseases which can affect other greenhouse plants.

Cucumbers

The season is drawing to a close — the plants are cleared at the end of the month. Until then water regularly, damp down on warm days and pick regularly.

Vegetables

Sow Carrot, Lettuce, Radish, Endive and Mustard & Cress.

Prick out Lettuce.

Harvest Capsicum, Aubergine, Radish, Mustard & Cress and Mushroom.

Fruit

Harvest Melon and Grape. Judging the right time to pick Grapes is not straightforward — the bunches must be left on the vine for a week or two or even a couple of months after the fruit appears ripe. See The Fruit Expert for details.

OCTOBER

There is much less work to do in the greenhouse now that the summer crops and summer heat have gone. No more daily waterings, no more constant syringing of floor and walls and no more Tomatoes and Cucumbers to look after. Chrysanthemums and Perpetual-flowering Carnations provide most of the colour and it is now time to start worrying about heating and insulation. The annual clean-up must take place in the September–November period — early October is an excellent time for this task. Complete the clean-up before bringing in the frost-sensitive plants for winter protection.

General Tasks

Heating now starts in the cool house — maintain a minimum night temperature of 42°–45°F. If frost is forecast you will have to protect tender specimens with matting.

●

Stop damping down — the extra humidity which was so necessary in the summer months is now no longer required. In fact moist air can pose a problem by encouraging grey mould. Some ventilation is therefore necessary, its purpose being to create fresh and moving air rather than to cut down the temperature.

●

Ventilate a little each day between mid-morning and early afternoon. Use the roof ventilators only. Close down at night, although you will have to leave a small gap if a paraffin stove is used. Do not ventilate on damp or foggy days.

●

Water with care — make sure that the pot requires watering before applying it. Do not splash the water about — keep it off the floor, staging, leaves and crown of the plants. Do this watering before midday which will allow time for splashes to dry before sunset.

●

Inspect the plants. Remove dead flowers and yellowing or diseased leaves. Put down slug pellets if slime trails or damaged foliage is seen. Spray if grey mould or whitefly has become a problem — do this spraying in the morning.

●

Make sure that all the half-hardy plants have been brought inside.

●

Insulation can be carried out this month in cold districts — leave this task until November or December in mild areas.

TEMPERATURE RECORD

Day	Minimum	Maximum

NOTES

On Display

Abutilon
Campanula
Canna
Capsicum annuum
Carnation
Chrysanthemum
Cyclamen
Fuchsia
Heliotrope

Impatiens
Jacobinia
Nerine
Pelargonium
Plumbago
Primula
Saintpaulia
Salpiglossis
Solanum capsicastrum

Plumbago capensis

Salpiglossis sinuata

NOTES

Bulbs

Plant the traditional spring-flowering bulbs — Tulip, Hyacinth, Narcissus, Snowdrop, Muscari, Crocus, Chionodoxa and so on for display in the greenhouse or living room.

Dry off Begonia, Hippeastrum, Gloxinia, Lily, Achimenes, Canna etc once flowering has finished.

Water and feed Lachenalia, Cyclamen and Freesia.

Prick out Cyclamen seedlings.

Pot Plants

Prick out last month's sowing of annuals for spring display. Pinch out the growing tips of older seedlings to induce bushiness.

Pot on Cineraria, Calceolaria and Schizanthus.

Reduce watering of established plants — avoid water-logging at all costs.

Cut Chrysanthemums and Perpetual-flowering Carnations for arranging indoors. Keep watch for grey mould and earwigs on Chrysanthemums.

Make sure that the last of the tender pot plants have been brought inside. Keep the compost almost dry.

Bedding Plants

Garden Pelargonium and Fuchsia which were potted up and brought inside last month for overwintering should be stored under the staging and kept quite dry. They will be brought back into growth next spring and bedded out again in May or June.

Pot on rooted cuttings.

Garden Perennials & Shrubs

Continue to take cuttings of evergreens. Always use a rooting hormone such as Bio Roota. Use a propagator or cover pot with a polythene bag — see page 35.

Dahlias should be lifted from the border when the first frosts have blackened the foliage. Complete this lifting by the end of the month. Cut down to 6 in. and label with the colour and name of variety. Gently fork out and shake off soil. Store the clumps of tubers in a peat-filled box after they have been left to dry upside down for a few days. Store the box under staging until the spring when the young shoots will be used as cuttings.

Tomatoes

Continue picking if plants were not lifted last month. Remove plants and containers when cropping stops.

Cucumbers

No work to be done this month.

Vegetables

Remove Aubergine and Capsicum plants when cropping stops.

Plant up seedlings sown last month.

Sow Lettuce.

Harvest Capsicum, Aubergine, Radish, Mustard & Cress and Mushroom.

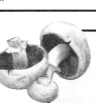

Fruit

Reduce watering. Ventilation is required for established Peach and Nectarine — these trees require cool and dry air in order for the wood to ripen.

Prepare ground for planting Peach, Nectarine, Apricot or Grape vine next month.

Harvest Grapes.

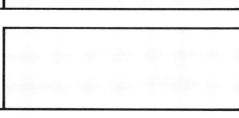

NOVEMBER

The Tomatoes have gone and November heralds the end of the autumn growing season. A quiet time in the greenhouse, but there is a reasonable amount of work to do if you are using the space properly. Pots will need careful watering and proper ventilation is a tricky job — there must be enough air movement to reduce the risk of disease but not enough to chill the plants. November is a suitable month for the annual clean-up — don't leave this essential task until the depths of winter.

General Tasks

Maintain a minimum temperature of 42°–45°F in the cool greenhouse if frost-sensitive plants are present. In a cold house it will be necessary to cover such specimens with matting if night frost is forecast.

●

If the day is dry and sunny, open a ventilator away from the wind. Close down the ventilator in mid-afternoon so the sun's heat will be conserved before nightfall. Keep the ventilators closed on damp or foggy days.

●

Try to keep the air on the dry side — don't splash the floor, staging or leaves when watering. Pots should be watered sparingly except for plants which are in flower.

●

Inspect the plants. Space out pots to ensure maximum illumination. Remove dead flowers and yellowing or diseased leaves. Spray if grey mould or whitefly has become a problem.

●

This is a good time for the annual clean-up. Choose a bright and dry day — begin work about mid-morning as there may be a lot to do. Place pots in a safe place in the garden — move tender types indoors. Remove rubbish from inside the house and scrub the staging and shelves with a garden disinfectant. Use a stiff brush to clean aluminium frames. Remove all traces of shading from the glass and clean thoroughly, both inside and out. If wood is unsightly paint with Bio Woody. Dig if you plan to grow in the border soil. When the clean-up is over bring back the plants from their temporary outing in the garden.

●

Clean-up time is an ideal opportunity for carrying out minor repairs and for insulating the house — see General Tasks for December on page 62.

TEMPERATURE RECORD

Day	Minimum	Maximum

NOTES

Zygocactus truncatus

On Display

Abutilon
Begonia
Browallia
Capsicum annuum
Carnation
Chrysanthemum
Cyclamen
Erica
Exacum

Impatiens
Jacobinia
Nerine
Pelargonium
Primula
Saintpaulia
Salvia
Solanum capsicastrum
Zygocactus

Capsicum annuum

Bulbs

Finish planting up the spring-flowering bulbs — include Tulip, Iris reticulata and Lily of the Valley.

Look at the bowls you have plunged outdoors. If shoots are about 1 in. high bring some inside to induce earlier flowering.

Pot Plants

Pot up cuttings of Pelargonium, Fuchsia, Heliotrope, Helichrysum, Campanula, Plumbago etc which were struck in autumn.

Bring in pots of Fuchsia, Hydrangea, Begonia and Pelargonium from outdoors — store under staging and keep the compost almost dry.

Pot up a few hardy plants from the garden for Christmas display — examples are Polyanthus and Helleborus niger.

Cut Chrysanthemums and Perpetual-flowering Carnations for arranging indoors. Keep watch for grey mould and earwigs on Chrysanthemums.

Bedding Plants

Pot on the hardy annuals which were sown in autumn for spring bedding — examples include Pansy and Sweet Pea. Pot on Pelargonium and Fuchsia cuttings for bedding out next year — see Pot Plants above.

Pack plants taken from hanging baskets into boxes containing slightly damp peat.

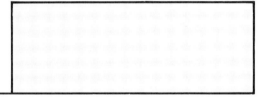

Garden Perennials & Shrubs

Perennials such as Chrysanthemum and Delphinium should be lifted from the border and packed into peat-filled boxes. Label and cut down to 4 in. before boxing, then place under the staging until the spring when the young shoots will be used as cuttings.

Bring tubs of tender shrubs and perennials (Agapanthus etc) into the greenhouse — prune as necessary.

Tomatoes   No work to be done this month.

Cucumbers   No work to be done this month.

Vegetables

Plant out into the border or into growing bags Lettuce seedlings raised from a September or early October sowing. A minimum of 45°F will be necessary. Plant out Mushroom spawn.

Harvest Lettuce and Mushroom.

Pot up and force Chicory. For instructions on how to do this see page 25.

Box up and force Rhubarb at the end of the month. Lift crowns of well-established plants from the open garden and leave exposed to frost. Then place crowns in a peat-filled box and cover with black polythene sheeting. Small and succulent shoots will be ready for pulling in about 4 weeks.

Lift from the garden and pot up Chives, Parsley and Mint for a supply during the winter months.

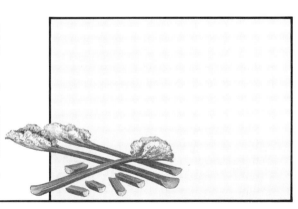

Fruit

Plant Peach, Nectarine and Apricot. Established bushes or fans should be ventilated during dry days — heat is not necessary.

Plant Grape vines. Prune established vines once all the leaves have fallen — see The Fruit Expert (page 91) for full instructions.

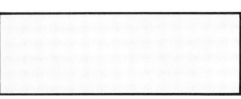

DECEMBER

The greenhouse owner reaps the benefit of earlier work this month. Pots of Cyclamen, Primula, Cineraria etc are brought into the living room for Christmas decoration — so are bowls of forced Narcissi and Hyacinths. In addition Christmas lunch can include home-grown Carrots, Mushrooms and Potatoes plus a Lettuce and Chicory salad. A satisfying month, then, but also a difficult one. December is not the coldest month, but it is the darkest one. This means that growth is sluggish and light is the controlling factor. Without supplementary lighting you should keep both the air and soil on the dry side and the temperature should be kept at less than 60°F.

General Tasks

Watch the temperature carefully. In a cool house aim for a minimum night temperature of 42°–45°F and a maximum day temperature of 55°–60°F. High temperatures lead to soft and lanky growth.

●

Some ventilation will be necessary to remove condensation and to keep the air moving. Do this job carefully or you will create plant-killing draughts and a dangerous drop in temperature. Avoid problems by following the instructions set out in the General Tasks section for November.

●

You must keep the soil rather dry at this time of the year if the plants are not in flower — this is especially true for Cacti, Succulents and Pelargonium. Only damp down the floor and staging if it is really necessary, and do this job in mid-morning.

●

Inspect the plants. Remove dead flowers and yellowing or diseased leaves. Spray if grey mould or whitefly has become a problem. Put down slug pellets if tell-tale shiny trails are seen.

●

This is the time to insulate the greenhouse, as the coldest weather has not yet arrived. The general principle is to put up an inner skin of transparent plastic close to the glass — this reduces illumination slightly but even a simple arrangement will cut fuel bills by 20–30 per cent. Tailor-made panels are offered by some greenhouse manufacturers, but the usual practice is to attach polythene sheeting to the sides of the house with drawing pins, staples or adhesive strip so that a ½–1 in. layer of air is trapped between glass and plastic. Alternatively you can use bubble polythene which has air trapped within it. Whichever method you use it is necessary to avoid blocking the ventilators.

●

Trim the wicks of paraffin heaters to prevent the production of plant-toxic fumes.

TEMPERATURE RECORD		
Day	Minimum	Maximum

NOTES

On Display

Azalea	Hippeastrum
Begonia	Hyacinth
Camellia	Impatiens
Capsicum annuum	Narcissus
Carnation	Pelargonium
Chrysanthemum	Primula
Cineraria	Saintpaulia
Cyclamen	Solanum capsicastrum
Freesia	Zygocactus

Cyclamen persicum

Narcissus Paperwhite

Bulbs

Bring in more bowls of bulbs from outside to hasten growth. The buds of forced bulbs will start to show colour this month — move the bowls into the living room for Christmas or New Year decoration.

Plant Lilies. Support stems of Freesia and Lachenalia.

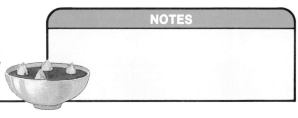

NOTES

Pot Plants

Move the Christmas pot plants to the warmest part of the greenhouse at the beginning of the month. Water carefully, adding a liquid feed. Take into the living room for the festive season — examples include Azalea, Cineraria and Primula.

Sow Campanula isophylla. Propagate Perpetual-flowering Carnations and stake Lorraine Begonias.

Bring in pot-grown Roses. Cut the stems to about 3–4 buds above the compost, or leave until next month.

This is a good time to get seed trays and pots ready for use in the New Year. Throw away broken ones — wash the remainder thoroughly with a garden disinfectant and stack neatly. Buy a multi-purpose compost.

Pot up shrubs for greenhouse decoration in spring. Examples include Forsythia, Hebe, Lilac and Weigela. A number of herbaceous perennials can be planted in pots. Suitable types are Lupin, Aquilegia, Delphinium and Gaillardia.

Bedding Plants

A quiet time here — sowing begins in January. Inspect the pots of autumn-sown hardy annuals. Make sure that they get maximum light and do not water unless the compost is distinctly dry on the surface.

Garden Perennials & Shrubs

Complete the cutting back of Chrysanthemums and Dahlias which were lifted and brought into the greenhouse last month. Keep these roots cool and fairly dry until they are brought into growth in January and February.

Tomatoes

The usual time for sowing Tomato seed is early March. However, in a heated greenhouse kept at a minimum night temperature of 50°–55°F, seed can be sown in a propagator in late December and planted out in early March for a June crop.

Cucumbers   No work to be done this month.

Vegetables

Sow Lettuce, Carrot, Mustard & Cress and French Bean — choose varieties recommended for growing under glass. Plant out October-sown Lettuce seedlings into the border or into growing bags.

Pot up and force Chicory — box up and force Rhubarb. See Vegetables section for November.

Harvest Lettuce, Carrot, Radish, Mushroom, Potato, Chicory and Rhubarb.

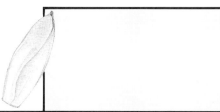

Fruit

Plant Peach, Nectarine, Apricot and Grape vine. Prune established Grape vines if not carried out last month — see The Fruit Expert (page 91) for full instructions.

These fruit trees do not make ideal companions for tender plants. Peach, Nectarine etc need unheated conditions and they also need to be ventilated freely on dry days.

CHAPTER 5

INDEX

Acknowledgements
The author wishes to acknowledge the painstaking work of Gill Jackson, Constance Barry, Jane Ducarreaux and John Woodbridge. Grateful acknowledgement is also made to Joan Hessayon, Linda Fensom, Jacqueline Norris, Angelina Gibbs, Pat Brindley and Harry Smith Horticultural Photographic Collection. Mike Standage and Deborah Achilleos prepared the paintings for this book.